Lutheran Charismatic Renewal Services

Richard E. Denny
Executive Secretary

Dear Lutheran Pastor,

This book is sent to you as a gift with the compliments of Lutheran Charismatic Renewal Services.

The "charismatic renewal" has been a growing phenomenon in most Christian churches since the early 1960's, and has had a significant impact among Lutherans. All three of the major Lutheran bodies in the United States have officially addressed themselves to the movement. At its national convention in Washington, D. C., in the fall of 1976, the ALC passed a resolution that urged..

That each district be encouraged to embark on an educational program for the clergy to assist them in understanding the Charismatic Movement, both objectively and subjectively, as to its beliefs and practices;

That pastors be encouraged to engage in dialogue with individuals or groups involved with the Charismatic Movement for better understanding and ministry to them.

This book by Larry Christenson, we believe, presents a truly Lutheran perspective on the charismatic renewal. It addresses itself both to the theological and the practical issues. We call your attention especially to Chapter Seven, where the sacrament of baptism is dealt with in a thoroughly Lutheran way. We hope that you will find real help in this book for better understanding the charismatic renewal, and its implications for the Lutheran ministry.

A <u>Study Guide</u> is available from LCRS as a companion to this book, so you can use it as a basis for group instruction and discussion. Additional copies of the book may be ordered directly from LCRS. The book retails at $2.95, the Study Guide at 10¢. A brief digest of the book, entitled, An Introduction to the Lutheran Charismatic Renewal" is also available at 20¢ a copy; it is designed for tract-type distribution.

Sincerely yours, in Christ,

Dick Denny

Dick Denny, Executive Secretary
for the LCRS Committee

DD bd

Box 14344 • University Station • Minneapolis, Minnesota 55414 • 612-636-7032

The Charismatic RENEWAL Among Lutherans

A Pastoral and
Theological Perspective

Larry Christenson

Published by
Lutheran Charismatic Renewal Services

Distributed by Bethany Fellowship, Inc., Minneapolis, Minnesota

Published by Lutheran Charismatic Renewal Services
Distributed to the trade by Bethany Fellowship, Inc.
6820 Auto Club Road, Minneapolis, Minnesota 55438

Printed in the United States of America

DEDICATION

This little handbook is dedicated to the people of Trinity Lutheran Church, San Pedro, California, who have walked with boldness in the things of the Spirit, with patience toward one another, with love for the Lutheran church.

TABLE OF CONTENTS

Larry Christenson graduated magna cum laude from St. Olaf College, Northfield, Minnesota, where he was elected to membership in Phi Beta Kappa. In 1959 he received the degree of Bachelor of Divinity from Luther Theological Seminary, St. Paul, Minnesota.

The author has been pastor of Trinity Lutheran Church in San Pedro, California, since 1960. He travels extensively as conference speaker in both the United States and Europe.

CHAPTER ONE

"The Distinctive Lutheran Contribution . . ."

In 1973 the charismatic renewal among Lutherans received a challenging word. It came from an unexpected source—two leaders in the Catholic Charismatic Renewal, Steve Clark and Ralph Martin.

They had invited me to visit them in Ann Arbor, Michigan, where they are coordinators of the "Word of God" community. While they themselves are Catholic, and have leadership responsibility in the Catholic Charismatic Renewal, their community is ecumenical, more than 50% Protestant, among which are a number of Lutherans.

This gave them a practical base of concern for the state of the charismatic renewal among Lutherans. They saw the need for Lutheran charismatics to get a clearer grasp of their own identity. Without this, Lutheran charismatics would tend to drift toward the Pentecostals on one side, or toward the Catholics on the other.

"That would be unfortunate," Steve Clark said, "because *the distinctive contribution of the Lutherans would be lost.*"

It surprised me at first that Catholics would be concerned to promote something distinctively Lutheran. I came to see, however, the wisdom of their words. Their approach to cooperation and unity among Christians was not "non-denominational," which so readily glosses over differences and reduces everything to the lowest common denominator. Unity achieved in this way tends to be shallow and one-dimensional. Their approach was truly ecumenical, which sees each tradition as having something special to contribute. Differences may be mutually enriching, or they may be items for discussion and exploration; they need not be divisive. We can respect, appreciate, and learn from one another's differences, even while the Spirit's patient work of forging a deeper unity is going on.

The ecumenical approach is slower than the non-denominational approach, but the results are deeper and more lasting. And it safeguards the treasures which the Lord has entrusted to each of the traditions.

This word found a response among leaders in the Lutheran wing of the charismatic renewal. They undertook a more active pastoral concern for relating the renewal to the heritage, theology, and structure of the Lutheran church. Through such things as the annual Lutheran Conference on the Holy Spirit, National Leaders' conferences, regional and local charismatic workshops, theological consultations, publications, and personal contacts, a growing unity and cohesiveness began to emerge in the Lutheran charismatic renewal. It took on a more distinctively Lutheran tone. Its impact on other segments of the charismatic renewal became more focused and precise. Other charismatic leaders began to refer to "what the Lutherans are saying ... the way it is working among the Lutherans." [1]

Segments of the Lutheran church still regard the charismatic renewal with suspicion, or with indifference. Its worship or theology or life-style do not strike them as harmonizing with the way Lutherans have traditionally done things. Many associate it with divisiveness. Lutheran church leaders and theologians have been wary of encouraging the movement or identifying with it in any official way. Official Lutheran statements, while noting some positive aspects of the renewal, have been thoroughly fenced around with questions, cautions, and criticisms. The Pentecostal stereotype persists, that people who go in for this kind of thing are over-emotional, theologically suspect, and vaguely uncultured.

Lutheran charismatics will have to live with this sterotype until they can live it down. In honesty it must be acknowledged that they have earned part of it by failing to take seriously their Lutheran culture and heritage. The early Lutheran movement was sometimes uncritical and unreflective about what it took over from classical Pentecostalism—biblical fundamentalism, doctrinal bias, cultural and ecclesiological traditions. While this was by no means true of all Lutheran charismatics, it was a contributing factor to some churches taking hardened positions against the charismatic renewal.

On the other hand, part of the stereotype has been hung around the neck of the renewal by sheer prejudice. Like all renewals, it brings the church under judgment, and the first reaction to this is not usually appreciation. Yet, the stereotypes will more readily give way where there is a patient effort to relate the charismatic renewal to the context of Lutheran culture.

The result of this effort, already coming into evidence, is twofold. Lutheran charismatics gain a new appreciation of their particular spiritual heritage. Their understanding and expression of the renewal becomes more authentically Lutheran. This brings something distinctive to the worldwide charismatic renewal.

At the same time, it opens the way for a positive witness to their own church. For if the charismatic renewal needs the distinctive contribution of the Lutherans, the Lutheran church just as certainly needs the distinctive contribution of the charismatic renewal.

Some Lutherans bridle at the suggestion that they have something to learn from the charismatic renewal. To admit it seems to imply a spiritual deficiency. And this brings another stereotype into play: the self-satisfied, complacent Lutheran. The Lutheran church, and especially its pastors and leaders, also has a stereotype to live down if it is to minister effectively to the charismatics in its fold.

The patient work of replacing stereotypes with mutual understanding and appreciation holds great promise for the fruitfulness of the charismatic renewal and for the renewal of the Lutheran church. The purpose of this little handbook is to outline the contribution which Lutherans and Lutheranism have to make to the charismatic renewal, and which the renewal offers to the Lutheran church.

CHAPTER TWO

Awakening

In the summer and fall of 1961 small groups of Lutherans, in scattered locations around the United States, began to have what later came to be known as "charismatic experience." [2] The focus of the awakening was on the reality and power of the Holy Spirit in one's life. It included the experience of some spiritual gifts which were uncommon among Lutherans, notably speaking in tongues, prophecy, and healing.

In 1963 the phenomenon began to spread among certain Lutheran groups in Germany,[3] since then to Lutherans in Scandinavia, Eastern Europe, Africa, Asia, Australia, and South America.[4] Within a dozen years the world's largest Protestant communion had felt the impact of the charismatic movement in virtually every segment of its worldwide membership.

The first general outbreak of charismatic activity among Lutherans occurred more-or-less simultaneously in California, Montana, and Minnesota. Within a decade, by conservative estimate, 10% of the Lutherans in the United States either testified to having had charismatic experience or were favorably disposed toward it.[5] The spread among Lutherans was paralleled in the other major historic denominations, notably, since 1967, among Roman Catholics. The religion editor of the *New York Times* called it "the most vital movement in American religion today." [6]

A spiritual awakening that has an impact upon the life of a million or more fellow Lutherans in the United States, not to mention the international and ecumenical dimensions, merits thoughtful consideration.

What has happened to these people who testify to having had charismatic experience? What kind of experience is it?

Here we let some Lutheran charismatics speak for themselves . . .

A Pastor

In December of 1963 I attended a meeting in a private home. There were forty people present, the majority of them Lutherans. The atmosphere of warmth, love, and friendliness was something highly unusual, especially in a big city setting. I had never met Lutherans quite like this. People were embracing each other and praising God with every other word. What could possibly have gotten to them? After a rousing singing of "A Mighty Fortress Is Our God," the meeting got under way. The leader spoke for some time. After his presentation he asked those who wanted "to receive the Spirit baptism" to raise their hands. I was sitting in the front row, wearing a clerical collar.

"Do you want to receive the baptism of the Spirit, Pastor?" he asked.

"Yes."

"Do you want to come forward for the laying on of hands?"

"No." (Before all these 'lay people'? He had to be kidding!)

Afterward I asked to hear a demonstration of "tongues." Suddenly there was a hum and babble throughout the room. Someone began to sing in the Spirit. It wasn't unpleasant, but it didn't make much sense either. All at once I thought I heard some vaguely understandable words coming through. I leaned over and listened carefully. A housewife sitting next to me just happened to be praying one of the Psalms in ecclesiastical Latin.

That night I got home very late. For some reason I was deeply disturbed. Had I heard Latin or not? Why were these Lutherans so different? Was God really pouring out the Spirit again in these days? After two big slugs of bourbon I drifted off into deep, but troubled sleep. And then I had a dream which indicated that the deepest layers of my personality had been uncovered. A secret, private chamber in that inner self had been broken into, and that which had been guarded and repressed all my life became explicit in the dream. Perhaps this is why it is so hard for some to surrender fully to God. God will not lie on the surface like seed on hard ground, but insists on getting down to the underside of our motivations where all our real willing and doing spring forth. Perhaps this is why some alcoholics and drug addicts "make it," and others do not. Before we can surrender to the power of God perhaps we need an authentic self to surrender. He will not settle for one of those "will-o-the-wisp," phantom, surface selves that come and go like Mayflies on a summer day. God wants to deal only with that deepest, hidden self, no matter how dark, ugly, or guilty it may be.

When I awoke, my head was still buzzing a little from the bourbon. I remembered that it was December 7. Twenty-two years before, on Sunday, December 7, 1941, I was pleasantly relaxing when the announcement came about the Japanese attack on Pearl Harbor. Nothing was the same ever again. Two years later, on December 7, 1943, I was an Army Air Force Cadet. I was scheduled to solo on the second anniversary of Pearl Harbor. Somehow I goofed and spoiled all the plans of my eager-beaver instructor. December 7, 1963, was scheduled to be the most dramatic of all.

Before the confirmation class, scheduled for 10:30 a.m., I went into the church for a few minutes of private prayer and devotion. The sanctuary never failed to impress me, no matter how many times I entered it. With balcony seating there was room for over a thousand worshipers. The magnificent pipe organ could rattle the giant stained glass windows which rose almost from the floor to the 55-foot ceiling. The tower held some twenty-odd tons of bells, and the narthex was a charming museum filled with expensive momentos of a glorious Germanic past. The thick walls and heavy carpet muffled the sound of the busy streets. It felt like home, the house of God, right in the middle of the world.

The pulpit was elaborately carved in highly polished red cherry wood with Martin Luther dominating the front. It was placed above and in back of the altar as a symbol of the high status Lutherans give to preaching. Entry to the pulpit was gained from a hidden panel in the side. Many a visiting preacher has to be rescued from the maze of the attached parsonage or from the church yard when he opens the wrong door. One Sunday I desperately chased a visiting dignitary all the way out into the street before I could guide him back to the pulpit.

Here, too, were the hidden scenes of many a fervent pastoral prayer, especially after I had begun to preach in Spanish as well as German and English every Sunday. "Oh, God! Let me out of here! I don't even know this language in which I am about to preach! Lord, you've got to take over! I have no message for this people!" Sometimes the prayers of the waiting congregation would carry me up those last few steps and the Spirit would whisper encouragement as I groped desperately for the right words.

Now, as I knelt before the communion rail, just to the right of the marble baptismal angel, I heard myself saying, "God, you and I are going to have it out this morning. Either you are going to be real, or I am going to quit. You can have the whole thing back—this church, my ministry, and me. I'm just going through the motions. I can't even stand to hear myself preach any more." At that moment I was convinced that hell for ministers was being forced to listen forever to tape recordings of their own sermons.

Suddenly a voice, clear and distinct, said, "The Gift is already yours; just reach out and take it." Obediently I stretched my hands toward the altar, palms up. I opened my mouth, and strange babbling sounds rushed forth. Had *I* done it? Or was it the Spirit? Before I had time to wonder, all sorts of strange things began to happen. God came out of the shadows. "He is real!" I thought. "He is here! He loves me!"

For the first time in my life I really *felt* loved by God. I laughed and danced for joy. The whole church was bathed in a soft, golden light. The world was turned inside out. Everything looked as fresh and new as the first morning of creation. Every cell and atom of my body tingled with the vibrant life of God. Every electron in my being clapped its hands and praised the Lord. "God, where have you been all this time? Were you locked behind that silly babble, or hidden under that desperate prayer of surrender? So near, and yet so infinitely far; so complex and yet so terribly simple ... how can we ever understand you? Give us *this* key, so that we can unlock you for the whole world."

Suddenly I wanted to run out on the street and tell everybody: "Stop the traffic! Stop the trains! listen! God is alive! He's really alive and real! He just told me back in the church!"

But there was a confirmation class waiting. When I floated in on that pink cloud, there was a sudden and unusual silence. They stared at me in silent wonder. Did it show? Was there a secret sign on my forehead, or perhaps an angel sitting on my shoulder? Did my face shine like that of Moses when he came down from the mountain? I, too, had talked face to face with God. Years later two members of the class told me that I had talked for ten minutes in a strange language they couldn't understand. They thought it might have been one of the many languages I was interested in. As a postscript, I should add that that was the only time in which the "tongue" got beyond conscious control.

For a few weeks I experienced a kind of euphoria that I had never known before. As I walked the streets I kept chanting, "I'm alive, I'm alive, God is real, He loves me, He loves me." Every bird and every breeze joined in the chant. The traffic and the trains were praising God, and every raindrop sparkled like a jewel in Cartier's window. The next week my wife and I attended a magnificent performance of Handel's *Messiah*. That was a foretaste of heaven. In my new joy I understood why, after this work literally flowed out of him, Handel could only weep. How glorious God truly is! And if praising God in heaven is anything like that December night, it's no wonder that we grow impatient and irritable with the things of earth! [7]

A Young Married School Teacher

In the last few years God has become more real and personal to me than He ever was before—and for this I thank and praise Him. This relationship has come in a number of ways; the gifts of the Spirit, however, were undoubtedly the impetus. From this initial contact with a God who would pour himself so freely upon His people, and fill them with a love of which they are incapable, I have grown in faith with each new example in the congregation and my own life that God is active among His people. The prayer groups have been a wonderful blessing, as have the Bible studies. My response has been a desire to be where Christ is, for He has become the ONE whom I love and worship. My life has become Christ's—Christ has become my life.

A Housewife, Mother of Six Children

I thank and praise God for making me truly aware of His wonderful love and the assurance of salvation—from changing a "have to" Christian into a "want to" Christian!—of a love of serving, not for myself as formerly but for the love of Jesus. I praise Him for the gift of His Holy Spirit which daily shows me the areas of my life that still need to be cleansed.

I thank and praise my Lord for all He has done in our family. He has brought two of our teenage children into a close and personal relationship with Him and given them the gift of His precious Holy Spirit.

The nourishment and fellowship in the congregation have been a tremendous blessing—we thank God for leading us to it.

A Pastor's Wife

At Bible camp, when I was sixteen, Jesus Christ

became a real person to me. I experienced a wonderful peace and joy. When I went home that weekend, I knew my life was different. After that I tried to live a Christ-centered life in our congregation, tried to do what Christ would want me to do. I had found a more worthy life goal than my previous one, which was to attend the university and have a yellow convertible.

I attended one of our Lutheran colleges, was active in campus religious activities, a senior chapel speaker. I married a fine Christian man, participated in a vital Lutheran congregation after our marriage, spent four years in activities at the seminary while my husband was in attendance, was blessed by many of the outstanding preaching ministries of our church.

I was not lacking in Lutheran heritage and experience. Yet I never learned really to pray. Through the years Jesus became distant and had very little claim on my heart—my mind, yes; my heart, no! I had realized that I couldn't do without Him, but I made Him do without me. And actually I had lost that peace that passes understanding, and the joy which the Holy Spirit produces.

The first time I ever heard anyone speak in tongues I knew immediately that this was the same Spirit which I had experienced fifteen years before. I knew that I could speak in tongues too; in fact I felt that if I opened my mouth, I would.

My reaction after that evening was mainly fear, fear of the thing itself—that God could be that real—but mostly fear of people. They would think of me as I had thought of others when "speaking in tongues" was only a phrase of words to me: "This is fanatical and repulsive!"

Two days later I was alone, resting, and a wave which I could feel rolled over me. There was a word in my mind which had no meaning to me. When

I spoke it, several other words came. But I clamped it off in fear, and did not speak in tongues anymore for two or three months.

During this time I was very disturbed. Most of the time the only prayer which I could honestly pray was: "Take my hand, dear Father, and lead Thou me." My final conclusion was that if I would reject this, I must reject all of my Christian experience as a figment of my imagination and a delusion. Thinking of life without Christ, I said, "Give me my delusions!" I prayed, "Lord, I believe. Help Thou my unbelief. I want only Thee, no matter what the price."

More than twelve years have passed since that first charismatic experience. While it began with speaking in tongues, it has gone on to revitalize the whole of my life in Christ. I can think of no price or honor which could persuade me to cancel out these years and go back to where I was before, spiritually. Although there has been testing and difficulties because of this experience, God has given me His assurance and inner peace—peace which the world cannot give and cannot take away.

"Let this mind be in you, which was also in Christ Jesus . . . he humbled himself and became obedient unto death" (Phil. 2:5, 8). Speaking in tongues has been an aid to me in humbling myself, and God has given me new power to be obedient. I have a greater realization of what "death of the self" means.

The most immediate and also the most lasting effect of this experience is that I want to pray and read the Bible. If I don't begin the day with prayer, I am uneasy. Reading the Bible gives me deep satisfaction and edification. God's guidance in my life is more clear to me. The work of God in the world is more evident to me.

All these things were beginning in me when I was converted, but I ran out of gas. I was unable to "abide in Christ." There is now an almost constant awareness of the presence of God in my life in a way which I knew only spasmodically or accidentally before.

Perhaps God knows that we need a sign again to give us power against the distractions and temptations of the world, and to keep us singleminded. I thank the Lord that He sent someone to tell me of this sign. If it would help others as it has helped me, they have the right to hear about it.

A High School Student

The Lord has blessed my life greatly during the last three years. He has given me the Holy Spirit and renewed strength to combat Satan. I can't see how anyone can say that God is dead. Just the fact of seeing my friends' lives change to the glory of God, and also the manifestation of His Spirit in my life and others, testify that God isn't dead but very much alive.

A Businessman

The Lord has blessed me with a renewal of the Holy Spirit. Many of the blessings are not yet completed, but only in the process, and many of the blessings I am probably still unaware of. However, I do have the confidence that I am growing in the Spirit and in God's will.

The gift of speaking in tongues came to me only after I had witnessed the effect it was having on my wife. It then was given to me after I had sought it in confession, prayer, and release. The gift came to me in song, and I still most often express it in this way.

Of course spiritual renewal and conformity to God's will are possible without the gift of speaking in tongues: They can be fruit of a dedicated Christian life. However, I must confess that until I experienced this gift they were not very evident in my life. I was, and had been, active in church activities and undoubtedly many would have said that I was living a truly Christian life. I can assure you I was trying, but there was something missing: *I* was trying to do God's work. There is now within me a new joy, a new vitality, a new desire and urgency. It is not *I*, but Christ in me. I am aware of this continually, and I thank God for it in prayers of tongues and in prayers of my understanding.

As to the overall effect, I would say this renewal of the Holy Spirit has awakened within me an awareness to the true blessing of Christ: His ministry, His death, His resurrection—our salvation. I have found a new desire to read God's Word, new understanding as I read and hear it preached. I have found a greater conviction of sin—mine and others. I have felt much more the urge to witness to others and the ability to do so seems to be increasing. I believe that more and more my desire is to put God's work first and to be truly dedicated to Christ.

A Lifelong Lutheran

I've known Jesus as my personal Savior as far back as I can remember. My parents loved the Lord and taught me this love early.

When I was a teenager, my Lutheran church (ALC) sent me to a Luther League Leadership Training School. There we learned that God wants us to totally give Him our lives and that He wants to fill us with His Holy Spirit. The theme song was—

Have Thine own way Lord, Have Thine own way,
Thou art the potter, I am the clay . . .

Each time we sang this song, I sang it as a prayer

to God with deep meaning. I'm sure it was at this time God filled me with His Spirit. I know I had received the Holy Spirit as a small child when I had received Jesus, just as the disciples did on Easter evening when Jesus breathed on them and said, "Receive the Holy Spirit" (John 20:22).

But, it was at this training school that, as a teenager, I was *filled* with the Holy Spirit. I'm sure of it because I had the evidence of the gift of tongues. (I believe a person can be filled with the Holy Spirit and not have tongues, but that tongues is *an* evidence of the infilling.)

But I was not aware I had tongues. It wasn't until a few years ago, when a Lutheran pastor prayed for me to receive tongues, that I remembered singing in tongues as a teenager. At that time, as a teen, I had no idea it was a gift from God. I wondered at the beauty of the "Lah-dah-dah-day" songs I was making up. But since I had no idea it was a special gift from God, I just forgot about it. Now that I know what it is and that it edifies (1 Cor. 14:4), I use this gift every day . . . especially since I know no gift of God does any good unless it is used.

A Housewife Who Prayed To Be Healed

I have been a Lutheran all my life and considered myself a Christian, although my faith at times was at a low ebb. When I look back on those years, I certainly realize what a poor Christian I have been.

A year ago I became seriously sick. I went through an operation that due to complications left me with a paralyzed leg. In spite of excruciating pain that persisted for weeks, I felt no bitterness, but was confident that God would answer my prayers and would heal me.

When I prayed, I never seemed to find enough

words for what I wanted to express. One day in my hospital room I realized that I was praying in a new language. The words came as fluently as if it had been my native language; yet it was not my native tongue, nor any of the other four languages I can speak. I felt a closeness to God that I had never before experienced. Although this was a surprise to me, I did not try to analyze the miracle, but accepted it as a gift from God to give me a more perfect communion with Him.

At the time I received this gift I did not know anything about "speaking in tongues." A week later, however, a friend read me an article in a magazine that told about it, and then I became eager to know of others whose experience was similar to mine.

The Bible became more meaningful to me. It was like a light had been turned on to give me better insight and understanding. God had, through the Holy Spirit, become a new reality to me.

In the course of a seven-week recuperation period God also answered my other prayer: The feeling and strength came back into my leg. I *walked* out of that hospital! Truly, He is a God who answers prayer.

My Own Testimony

I am a Lutheran, born and bred.

When I was about ten years old, our family went visiting relatives one weekend. My parents found out that the Lutheran church in this little Iowa town had a whole raft of baptisms and confirmations scheduled for that Sunday; the service would last until 2:00 p.m. They decided to go to the Methodist church instead. But they didn't brief us children ...

We got inside the church and were being ushered down the aisle when I noticed that something was different. Maybe it was the absence of altar hangings, or maybe the minister was dressed in a suit rather than a robe—I don't remember. But something mightily distressed me, because I blurted out: "This isn't a Lutheran church!" My mother went crimson and leaned down to hush me up. But I refused to be placated. Louder still I insisted: "This isn't a Lutheran church! I'm getting out!" I made resolutely for the door with my chagrined parents tracking after me.

That was my first ecumenical adventure. Neither my parents nor my home church had drilled a rabid Lutheran loyalty into me. I imagine it was just the natural reckoning of a child who had never been in any other church.

My later contacts with other denominations have been somewhat more friendly and fruitful than the first! Indeed, the Lord has blessed me in many ways through the people and ministry of other denominations. And yet that childhood experience has a point, for still, as an adult, I hold a deep sense of love and loyalty for the Lutheran church.

When I was a senior at our seminary—just a few months short of graduation—I began to feel a strange uneasiness in my soul. I found myself drawn to the book of Acts. I read and re-read the adventures of the early church. I sensed something in the experience of those early Christians which was missing in my own life. It was hard to put my finger on it, because my theological training tended to supply a ready answer for most of my questions. But the uneasiness continued. It centered around the power and intimate sense of direction which the early disciples seemed to have. These elements seemed lacking in my own experience—indeed, in the experience of much of the church, as I had known it.

I remember doing a paper for one of my dogmatics professors, the late Kent Knutson, in which I said, "One can hardly read the book of Acts on the one hand and a recent history of some Christian denominations on the other without some grave tremblings: *Where is the power*?

"Has the Holy Spirit withdrawn, of a purpose, from His more dynamic manifestations? Or have we, perhaps, quenched the free operation of the Spirit by our unbelief—by our blind clinging to the sacred dogma of Scientific Causality?

"Let us be quit of the nonsense that in 'de-mythologizing' the miraculous or supernatural elements of Scripture we succeed in 'interpreting' them—in getting at their 'true meaning.' Above and beyond any particular *Weltanschauung* there are canons of simple honesty, which were the same in the first century as they are today. When we de-mythologize the paralogical manifestations of the Spirit—miracles, healings, tongues—we do not 'interpret' Peter or Paul or Luke: We simple call them liars." Dr. Knutson penned-in the comment: "A spirited defense of the Spirit!"

I found myself going back to some of my notes and textbooks on the doctrine of the Holy Spirit, which I had studied two years earlier. One writer seemed to put into words the very thoughts which I was personally experiencing:

> We shall never rightly understand the essential being of the New Testament *Ecclesia* if we do not take fully into account the paralogical revelations of the Spirit . . . People draw near the Christian community because they are irresistibly attracted by its supernatural power . . . Theologians not only undervalue the dynamic power of the Holy Ghost, but often simply know nothing of it. With them the not unreasonable fear of an excess of enthusiasm of the paralogical has certainly had the effect of causing the Apostle's injunction, 'Quench not the Spirit' to

be disregarded, and of confining attention to his
warnings against the overvaluation of this paralogical, dynamic element.[8]

Something *was* missing in my Christian experience. I knew it. I could feel it. Yet I couldn't put
my finger on it.

The first answer to my uneasiness came through
learning about the revival of the ministry of healing
within the Episcopal church. I became acquainted
with the books of Agnes Sanford, Don Gross, Alfred
Price, Emily Gardiner Neal, et al. This seemed to
answer part of my quest: it made real and contemporary the element of power, the *dunamis,* so evident
in the book of Acts.

I attended several healing missions at local Episcopal churches. A belief in divine healing took firm
root in my own personal faith, and later in my ministry. There are many things about it which still puzzle
me, but Scripture leaves me no doubt that I shall
pray for the sick with the faith that "the Lord
will raise them up." (See James 5:14.)

At a clinic for Pastoral Care in December 1960,
I discovered that a number of people involved in
the ministry of healing were also experiencing some
of the other manifestations of the Spirit described
by St. Paul in 1 Corinthians 12—yes, even this strange
business of "tongues."

One rather amusing incident ensued. I was sitting
in a small dining room with three other men—an
Episcopalian layman, a Four-Square Gospel minister, and a Baptist minister. Just making conversation, I said, "You know, I understand there's more
of this speaking in tongues going on than a lot of
people realize." They nodded, and exchanged glances
with one another. As it came out in our conversation,
all three of them had spoken in tongues—one for
the first time that very morning! As we were sitting

there, a woman leaned her head in the door and
spoke to us. I recognized her accent as German.
(I had spent a year in Germany after graduation
from seminary.) I stood up and spoke to her: *"Bitte,
nehmen Sie Platz!"* She reared back and said,
"Where did you learn to speak fluent German?"
The Episcopalian layman riveted his eyes on me,
and I saw what was going through his mind; he
thought the Spirit had fallen on me right then and
there, simply through our talking about it. I laughed
and told him, "No, sorry; I learned that the hard
way."

But a seed had been planted. I wasn't particularly
eager about speaking in tongues. Frankly, I didn't
see much *purpose* in it. Yet I was open to it. And
then I found that some of that old uneasiness began
to stir inside me again. So I laid it before the Lord
in prayer and said, "Lord, if this is something you
want me to have, then show me—in your own way,
in your own time."

The Lord's answer came in a simple, unspectacu-
lar way: An elderly Norwegian lady—formerly a
member of the Hauge Lutheran Synod, now a member of the Foursquare Gospel Church in San Pedro—
called me up one day and asked if she might invite
some of our people to a revival they were having.
As it turned out, I was the one she was inviting.
I had a free evening the following Thursday and
decided it would be good relaxation to hear somebody
else preach for a change!

The evangelist, Mary Westberg, was speaking on
the gifts of the Spirit, out of 1 Corinthians 12. The
Lord spoke to me in that sermon. I went up to her
afterward, thanked her for the message, and said
I would appreciate her prayers: I wanted a more
Spirit-filled ministry. She asked if I had received
the "baptism." I gave her a puzzled look. "The bap-

tism with the Holy Spirit," she explained. "Well, I don't know," I answered, a little uncertainly, "not as a definite experience, at any rate." This was unfamiliar terminology to me. (It was August 1961; the charismatic movement had not yet begun in the Lutheran church.)

She and her husband offered to pray with me. They said that I should simply yield my tongue to the Lord and He would give me a new language—an "unknown tongue"—with which to praise Him. My mind was racing with a thousand questions, doubts, uncertainties, fears. Overriding all else was the fear of "faking" anything—of letting my desire for a blessing from the Lord run out ahead of His Spirit. They prayed and I prayed, but nothing demonstrable happened.

That night, sometime after midnight, I woke from a light sleep, sat bolt-upright in bed, and found an "unknown tongue" hovering on my lips. Fully aware of what I was doing, I spoke a sentence in the tongue—and promptly fell back to sleep. I woke up in the morning with a clear recollection of the experience, though at first I thought I might only have dreamed it. Later in the week, however, I experienced this new kind of prayer when I was fully awake. It has been a valuable part of my prayer life ever since.

That is how it began with me—an interest in healing and the experience of speaking in tongues.

These initial events were a kind of doorway into a new dimension of spiritual awareness. Since then I have known the reality of Christ in a new way. Before, it was primarily my thoughts that were affected, my system of ideas. Now it is my life and actions, and my deeper attitudes and feelings as well. Faith has taken on a more personal quality. Prayer has become a cornerstone of daily life. The Word of God has gained new power to shape my thought and action. I have come into more deeply committed relationships with other Christians. Concern for the upbuilding of the church, and for her witness in the world, is not simply an ideal, nor a task; it is a daily conversation with the Lord of the Church. All of this I attribute to the work of the Spirit.

I was once asked, "Couldn't all this have happened without a charismatic emphasis, without healing and speaking in tongues?"

Certainly these elements are not the main thing. But neither am I ready to dismiss them as irrelevant or dispensable. Spiritual renewal, after all, is not a "something" which we can manipulate at will. It is a particular shape and vitality which Jesus gives to our relationship with Him. I believe that behind this renewal, and including the renewal of spiritual gifts, lies a sovereign determination of God. I do not speculate whether renewal might have happened in some other way. That would be a little like wondering whether one might have had just as good a marriage if he had married someone else. Life is made up of our real choices and experiences, not theoretical possibilities. I am thankful for the deepening of spiritual life, and the experience of spiritual gifts, which has come to me in the charismatic renewal.

And I do not believe it is a purely private matter. I believe that what I and others have experienced is part of a great initiative of the Holy Spirit throughout the whole church.

When 10,000 Roman Catholic charismatics celebrated Pentecost in Rome, in 1975, a leading Catholic theologian said, "This marks a new epoch in the history of the Roman Catholic Church." [9] In the charismatic renewal we are participating in a move of the Spirit which, in its scope and impact, will have historic impact upon the life of the church.

CHAPTER THREE

"The Lord and Giver of Life"

The charismatic renewal lays special emphasis upon the person and work of the Holy Spirit. It has helped stimulate a fresh interest in this neglected[10] aspect of the Christian faith. It is recording new experience for the church to understand and interpret. It brings freshness to the use and understanding of Scripture and poses new questions to the interpretation of the text.[11] A greater understanding and appreciation of the Holy Spirit is one of the positive benefits which the charismatic renewal is helping bring about in the church.

Terminology

The word "charismatic" is derived from the Greek *charismata*.[12] The root word is *charis*, which means "grace." *Charismata*, therefore, could be translated literally as "engracements," [13] though the usual translation is "spiritual gifts." It is helpful, however, to keep in mind the root meaning, for these gifts are indeed *of grace*, given not earned.

According to this fundamental meaning of the word, every Christian is charismatic, being graced by God to function as a member of the Body of Christ. (See 1 Cor. 12:7; Rom. 12:5-6.)

Since 1960 the word charismatic has taken on a specialized meaning. We speak of the "charismatic movement" or "charismatic renewal." We refer to certain Christians as "charismatic." (The term "neo-Pentecostal" is equivalent, though not as widely used.) Used in this way the term "charismatic" takes on *historical* connotation: The charismatic renewal is an identifiable historical phenomenon. While it has some connections with classical Pentecostalism,[14] it is nevertheless historically distinct, a widespread movement within the historic denominations which began around 1960. A "charismatic" in this sense is someone who has chosen to identify himself with this movement. He shares in the experiences and socialization which characterize it; he reads the literature, goes to the meetings, and becomes engaged with elements of the theology and life-style emerging in the movement.[15]

The use of the term "charismatic" to identify this movement is, of course, not accidental. It is related to the fundamental meaning of the word; the movement has laid special stress on the gifts of the Holy Spirit.

This specialized use of the word charismatic seems to be here to stay. From popular newspaper articles to official church documents, reference to "charismatics" and "charismatic renewal" is consistent, and relatively unambiguous.[16] We need to recognize, as one Catholic charismatic has pointed out, that "usage comes from the people. It cannot be imposed by an academy." [17] This is especially true in the case of a popular movement.

Nevertheless, both those within and outside the charismatic movement need to recognize that this specialized use of the term charismatic is descriptive, not exclusive. It is akin to a term like "The *Evangelical* Lutheran Church." It describes a positive emphasis or concern; it should not be understood as an exclusive claim upon the territory occupied by that word.

Thus the term "charismatic" designates this particular renewal movement within the church which has a certain emphasis or focus, and the people who are identified with it.

Doctrine and Experience

What has emerged in the charismatic renewal is not a reformulation of the doctrine of the Holy Spirit. On the contrary, charismatics tend to affirm with enthusiasm historic formulations of the doctrine. At a charismatic conference in Minneapolis, during a time of free worship, one of the participants broke into a spontaneous chant of the well-known words from Luther's small catechism—

> I believe that by my own reason or strength I cannot believe in Jesus Christ, my Lord, or come to him. But the Holy Spirit has called me through the Gospel, enlightened me with his gifts, and sanctified and preserved me in true faith, just as he calls, gathers, enlightens and sanctifies the whole Christian church on earth and preserves it in union with Jesus Christ in the one true faith. In this Christian church he daily and abundantly forgives all my sins, and the sins of all believers, and on the last day he will raise me and all the dead and will grant eternal life to me and to all who believe in Christ. This is most certainly true.[18]

What charismatics are bringing forth is not a new statement of the doctrine, but a fresh experience of it. The experience has served to heighten their appreciation of historic Christian teaching on the Holy Spirit. The Spirit is no longer a "vague, oblong blur," as one man put it; He is the divine person of the creeds, the Lord and giver of *life,* the revealer of Christ, the One who guides us into truth.

This accent on the person of the Holy Spirit is linked to the experience of receiving or being filled with His presence. Precisely because He is a person, He must be received. The effectual presence of the Holy Spirit cannot be assumed simply because a person agrees to correct doctrine. It is possible to hold the doctrine on the Holy Spirit, yet not experience His presence and power. The doctrine must find expression in personal experience. This is a fundamental perception of the charismatic renewal.

CHAPTER FOUR

The Gift of the Holy Spirit

Peter's Pentecost sermon in Acts ended with a call to repentance, an invitation to baptism, and the promise of "the gift of the Holy Spirit" (Acts 2:38).

The gift of the Holy Spirit is the Spirit himself. It is the personal presence of God that fills the believers. He does manifest himself in dynamic ways. Nevertheless, it is himself, not merely His dynamisms, which constitute the "gift." *

According to classic Christian teaching, the Holy Spirit is received when one becomes a Christian. "Any one who does not have the Spirit of Christ does not belong to him" (Rom. 8:9).

All Christians have God's Spirit (Ro. 8:9, I Co. 2:12, I Co. 3:16, Gal. 4:6, I Jn. 3:24). All they that belong to the Body, Christ, are baptized with one Spirit, namely, the Holy Spirit.[19]

The gift of the Holy Spirit is a part of the gift of salvation. The experience of the Holy Spirit comes as one reckons upon this fact and puts it into practice.[20]

The church bodies which developed out of the

---

*Grammatically, in Acts 2:38 we do not have the subjective genitive (the gift which is given by the Holy Spirit) but the genitive in apposition, i.e., "The gift *which is* the Holy Spirit."

Pentecostal revival in the early years of the 20th century, generally known as *classical Pentecostals,* had their theological roots in the Wesleyan-Holiness tradition. In this tradition there had developed the idea that the gift of the Spirit is received through a second experience, following salvation. Classical Pentecostalism used this as the basic model for explaining its experience of the Holy Spirit. Its teaching on the subject included these elements—

(1) One receives the Holy Spirit in an experience subsequent to conversion or regeneration.

(2) The term used to designate this experience is "baptism with the Holy Spirit."

(3) The "initial evidence" of baptism with the Holy Spirit is speaking in tongues.[21]

(4) Baptism with the Holy Spirit opens the door for believers to receive various gifts of the Spirit, which empower them for mission.[22]

Classical Pentecostals linked baptism with the Spirit to the gift of speaking in tongues. This was the only new feature which they added to the Wesleyan-Holiness teaching which had developed in the second half of the 19th century.[23]

The two-stage view of classical Pentecostalism (conversion + baptism with the Holy Spirit) was widely used as a theological model in the charismatic renewal during the early 1960s. By the end of the decade, however, another view, more akin to the historic view, was emerging. This could be characterized as an "organic view" of the Spirit's work.

Among churches with more of a sacramental tradition (primarily Lutheran and Roman Catholic) charismatic experience has come to be seen as an outgrowth or actualization of the Spirit's work, which began when one was first grafted into Christ. This organic view is being used more and more widely as a theological model in the charismatic renewal.[24] It stands in continuity with the historic Christian understanding of one's growth in the Spirit and His gifts.

It understands the kind of experience which people are having in the charismatic renewal as a manifestation of Christian growth. Lutheran theologian William Lazareth described a charismatic's experience as "a particularly dramatic form of sanctification." [25] It marks a progression in one's life as a Christian, not an event by which one becomes a Christian. Understood in this way it does not present us with any great theological innovation; it accords with categories of historic Christianity.

This organic view understands the gift of the Holy Spirit, which is the Spirit himself, as being given to all Christians. To divide Christians into those who "only have salvation" and those who "have the Spirit" is unbiblical.[26] There is no formal "second stage" in the Christian life,[27] though there will be distinctive experiences. Thus, on the one hand, the "two-stage" theological model (conversion + baptism with the Spirit) is being replaced with the more historic "organic" view.

On the other hand, however, the distinctive experiential expectation of the Wesleyan-Holiness-Pentecostal tradition remains a vital part of the charismatic renewal. A distinct experience of personal renewal in the Holy Spirit continues to be a normal occurrence in the renewal. And while there is no doctrine of speaking in tongues as the "initial evidence of baptism with the Holy Spirit," nevertheless the experience of tongues, as well as other spiritual gifts, is expected and is in fact widespread.[28]

Lutherans have traditionally understood the gift of the Holy Spirit in terms of its essential purpose, which is to apply to the believer the benefits of Christ's suffering, death, resurrection, ascension, session at the right hand of the Father, and the promise of His coming again.

Neither you nor I could ever know anything of Christ or believe in him or take him as our Lord, unless these were first offered to us and bestowed on our hearts through the preaching of the Gospel by the Holy Spirit. The work is finished and completed, Christ has acquired and won the treasure for us by his sufferings, death, and resurrection, etc. But if the work remained hidden and no one knew of it, it would have been all in vain, all lost. In order that this treasure might not be buried but put to use and enjoyed, *God has caused the Word to be published and proclaimed, in which he has given the Holy Spirit to offer and apply to us the treasure of salvation.*[29]

Two points stand out in this paragraph from Luther's Large Catechism: The gift of the Holy Spirit is given—

(1) *Through* the proclamation of the Word;

(2) *In order* to offer and apply to us the treasure of salvation.

The gift of the Holy Spirit is thus inseparably linked with the Word and with Christ. These are the norms by which we interpret and evaluate the working and the experience of the Holy Spirit in a believer's life. Everything depends upon "the preaching of the gospel by the Holy Spirit." [30]

Lutherans would concur with the historic view of how one receives the Holy Spirit. They do not see the gift of the Holy Spirit being given at some "second stage" in the Christian life, but rather at the very beginning, in connection with baptism.[31]

Baptism, however, is not understood as a one-time bestowal of the Holy Spirit, but as an event which initiates an ongoing work of the Spirit. Luther calls this ongoing work of the Spirit a "spiritual baptism" which continues throughout life.

> The sacrament of baptism is quickly over. But the spiritual baptism, the drowning of sin, which it signifies, lasts as long as we live. . . . Similarly the lifting up out of the baptismal water is quickly done, but the thing it signifies—the spiritual birth and the increase of grace and righteousness—even though it begins in baptism, lasts until death, indeed, until the Last Day. Then only shall we be truly lifted up out of baptism and be completely born.[32]

This lifelong "spiritual baptism" includes the whole scope of one's life in Christ, including charismatic experience.[33] This is how traditional Lutheranism would interpret the kind of experience people are having in the charismatic renewal.[34] It is a special awakening to the reality and power of the Holy Spirit and His gifts, which has its roots in baptism, and will have its final consummation at the Last Day.

CHAPTER FIVE

Faith, Baptism, and the Manifestation of the Spirit

According to Acts,* after Pentecost the gift of the Holy Spirit is never separated from baptism. Luke does not contrast Christian water baptism with Spirit baptism, but he joins them.[35] Baptism is the objective event by which one is initiated into the church, the people of God.

Clustered together with baptism is the response of faith and the manifestation of the Holy Spirit, seen as a unity (Acts 2:38; see also Gal. 3:2, 26, 27; Tit. 3:5; Rom. 8:9). It is this organic whole which constitutes Christian initiation, and as a whole it is the Lord's gracious and sovereign work: He imparts faith, authenticates baptism, and confers the gift of

---

* A thorough examination of the doctrine of the Holy Spirit would need to consider a wider spectrum of Scripture than Acts. Our purpose in this book, however, is to speak to specific issues raised by the charismatic movement, and that is the reason we focus our biblical investigation on Acts. In the charismatic movement, as in classical Pentecostalism, the interpretation of Acts has been pivotal to understanding and explaining the gift of the Holy Spirit. It is here that we can recognize both the value of the charismatic contribution and the areas where exegetical and theological correction is needed.

the Holy Spirit. The Spirit is received in baptism where received in faith.

Acts 2:38, by its placement in Luke's narrative, becomes virtually a paradigm for Christian initiation—

Repent,

Be baptized,

Receive the gift of the Holy Spirit.

Baptism here is seen at the center of Christian initiation, the objective event by which one is brought into Christian life and fellowship.

It may be assumed that the 3000 converts on the day of Pentecost received the Holy Spirit, as Peter had just promised. The terse description of their response, however, mentions simply their baptism: "Those who received his word were baptized" (2:41).

Likewise, the Ethiopian eunuch responded to the teaching of Philip by saying, "See, here is water! What is to prevent my being baptized?" (8:37). Saul's response to the visit of Ananias was that "he rose and was baptized" (9:18). When the Spirit fell on the household of Cornelius, Peter immediately responded, "Can anyone forbid water for baptizing these people who have received the Holy Spirit just as we have?" (10:47). The response of Lydia and of the Philippian jailer to the preaching of Paul ended with them being baptized, together with their households (16:15, 33).

In 19:1-6 we have the incident of Paul encountering some Ephesian disciples who had not received the Holy Spirit, had not even heard that there was a Holy Spirit. Immediately Paul inquired concerning their *baptism*. When he discovered that they had only been baptized with John's baptism, he declared to them that what John had promised had now been fulfilled in Jesus, and he proceeded to administer Christian baptism. He then laid his hands on them, and they received the Holy Spirit. This text illustrates the apostolic consciousness of an organic connection between baptism and the gift of the Holy Spirit.

Luke's emphasis on baptism does not diminish the place given to faith, or the reception of the Spirit. On the contrary, it takes these things for granted; they are for Luke normally inseparable. Repentance, baptism, forgiveness of sins, faith, the reception of the Spirit—in whatever order or manner they may be experienced—are a unity.[36]

While faith, baptism, and the gift of the Holy Spirit form an organic whole,[37] there can be variety in the order in which they occur in personal experience. This is especially evident in regard to the relation between baptism and the manifestation of the Holy Spirit: Sometimes the gift is manifested more-or-less *simultaneously* with baptism (19:5-6), sometimes a period of time *after* baptism (8:14-17), sometimes *before* baptism (10:44-48). Thus, while the gift of the Holy Spirit is united with baptism, its manifestation may be distinct from baptism.

In 8:14-17 we have the case of Samaritans who had believed, but they had not yet received the Holy Spirit. They had only been baptized. This is a notoriously difficult passage to interpret. Some think the faith of the Samaritans was defective, and that explains why the Spirit was not given.[38] Another view is that the Lord delayed the giving of the Spirit until the apostles came, in order to show them that the gospel was meant also for the Samaritans.[39] Pentecostals see this text as supporting their doctrine of "two stages" in Christian initiation: conversion, followed by baptism with the Holy Spirit.[40]

This was in any case an irregular happening, and therefore cannot be used as a basis for formulating doctrine or practice.[41] The "not yet" and "only" in these verses suggest that Luke understood this as an unusual occurrence: faith, baptism, and the manifestation of the Holy Spirit normally came together in the apostolic community. When, on this occasion, it happened otherwise, the apostles took special measures on behalf of the new converts. "They prayed for them . . . then they laid their hands on them and they received the Holy Spirit" (8:15, 17).

The apostles, in going down to Samaria, recognized two coordinate facts—

(1) Faith, baptism, and the manifestation of the Holy Spirit belong together.[42] When baptism does not lead to the manifestation of the Spirit, steps should be taken to rectify the matter.

(2) Faith, baptism, and the manifestation of the Holy Spirit may be distinct from one another. It is the sovereign Lord, and not any mechanistic process, which links them together. Baptism does not magically impart the Spirit.[43]

A similar irregularity is evidenced in 10:44-48. While Peter preaches to a group of Gentiles in the household of Cornelius, the Holy Spirit falls on them. The bestowal of the Spirit is a sovereign act of the Lord, prior to and distinct from baptism. Peter nevertheless recognizes that faith, baptism, and the coming of the Spirit belong together and hence calls for their immediate baptism.

In Acts, the decisive event for the individual is to move from the company of the unbaptized to the company of the baptized. Clustered around this event will be one's personal response of faith and manifestations of the Holy Spirit. These are normal accompaniments to baptism. They may be described in some detail (10:30-46), alluded to sketchily (9:17-18), or simply assumed (2:48).

Thus faith, baptism, and the manifestation of the Spirit presuppose one another, yet they are distinct from one another. Both the unity and the distinction are presided over by the sovereign and gracious Lord.

Jesus tied the promise of the Holy Spirit to the mission of the church. "You shall receive power when the Holy Spirit has come upon you; and you shall be my witnesses in Jerusalem and in all Judea and Samaria and to the end of the earth" (Acts 1:8). Thus each believer who is united with the people of God, the church, is empowered by the Spirit to share in the church's mission. This is the principle thrust of Luke's teaching on the Holy Spirit, as presented in Acts.

The linking of the gift of the Holy Spirit to baptism underscores the personal character of the gift. The Holy Spirit is not a vague spirit of togetherness in the early church. He is given to each believer, personally and individually.

Nevertheless, while the Spirit is received by individual believers, the receiving is not individualistically oriented. One's receiving of the Holy Spirit is also a being received into the people of God. "They devoted themselves to the apostles' teaching and fellowship, the breaking of bread and prayers" (2:42). The personal receiving of the Holy Spirit is inseparable from one's incorporation into the saved and serving community.

CHAPTER SIX

Baptism with the Holy Spirit

A distinguishing mark of the charismatic renewal has been a widespread and distinctive experience which initially focuses upon the person and gifts of the Holy Spirit. The Anglican archbishop of Cape-town, William Burnett, characterized it as "an experience that is parallel to Pentecost." [44] The term most commonly used to designate this experience is "baptism with the Holy Spirit."

The biblical use of this term (always in its verbal form) is well known. It refers—

(1) To the messianic ministry of Jesus, who would baptize with the Holy Spirit (Matt. 3:11, Mark 1:8, Luke 3:16, John 1:33). The paradigm for baptism with the Holy Spirit is the baptism of Jesus, the setting in which the prophecy was given. [45] As Jesus came to John the Baptist to be baptized in the Jordan, a Christian comes to Jesus the "Baptizer" to be baptized with the Holy Spirit.

The use of the term has undoubtedly contributed to a strong Christ-centered emphasis in the charismatic renewal. The baptism with the Holy Spirit is understood not as an autonomous experience, but as proceeding from an encounter with Jesus. [46]

(2) To the day of Pentecost (Acts 1:5), and, by

extension, to the event in the household of Cornelius (Acts 11:16). In both of these instances believers are baptized with the Holy Spirit.

Our purpose in this chapter is to describe as accurately as possible the experience that people in the charismatic renewal call "baptism with the Holy Spirit." We are not articulating a normative doctrine on the matter. The biblical witness does not present a spelled-out doctrine on baptism with the Holy Spirit. It describes the experience of people who are baptized with the Holy Spirit in particular circumstances.

The description of the biblical experience has some parallels with the experience people are having today. On the one hand, therefore, we recognize that the present-day experience is not foreign or contrary to Scripture. On the other hand, however, we realize that doctrine rests on clear apostolic teaching, not simply on the description of events. (The doctrine of the resurrection does not rest merely on the description of the event, but on the Bible's clear teaching concerning it.)

Thus our consideration of the baptism with the Holy Spirit is meant to be essentially descriptive of what is happening today, not normative of what is supposed to happen at all times and places. This does not at all mean that it is an optional issue, either for the church or for an individual Christian. Rather, it forces us to ask the right kind of questions. The question is *not*, "Is baptism with the Holy Spirit laid down as an absolute doctrine in the Bible?" The questions, rather, would be in this vein: "Is the experience that many people testify to evidence of a genuine visitation of the Holy Spirit? As I hear and see it described, what kind of response does God look for from our church, or from me, personally? Am I truly open to the full range of what the Spirit wants to manifest in our church, or through me?"

While the experience of individuals will vary considerably, five elements could be cited that broadly characterize what people call baptism with the Holy Spirit:

(1) The experience usually occurs in the context of prayer, either private or corporate, usually after consciously asking for the blessing.

(2) The focus of one's prayer is upon a fullness or release of the Holy Spirit in one's life. The assumption is that one already has the Spirit, for without the Spirit one is not a Christian (Rom. 8:9). Thus the seeking is not with a view to becoming a Christian, but to receiving power to live the Christian life more effectively and fruitfully—to live under the lordship of Christ, to the glory of God, in the power of the Holy Spirit. The focus, therefore, is Trinitarian.

(3) The expectation is that one will receive a fresh release or bestowal of the Holy Spirit which will be marked and manifest. The expectation involves a sense of deep and long-range commitment, which distinguishes it from one's daily prayers for the help or guidance of the Spirit. For many it has the impact of *initiation* into a consciously Spirit-filled, Spirit-led life (which may partly explain the use of the term "baptism" in this regard).

(4) Those who pray for the filling of the Spirit, in the context of the charismatic renewal, usually speak in tongues, either at once or sometime afterwards. For some, another gift such as healing or prophecy may accompany the initial experience, but this is less common.

(5) The issue of the experience is a vitalization of one's faith, which may express itself in a variety of ways. For many it marks a turning point in their Christian life which is like a new beginning.

It is important to point out that neither in the Bible nor in present-day experience can baptism with the Spirit be properly understood as a "second baptism." There is only one baptism (Eph. 4:5). Baptism with the Holy Spirit is not separate from Christian baptism, but integrally united it. What people are experiencing in the charismatic renewal, as one Roman Catholic bishop has put it, is "a flowering or actualization of baptismal grace." [47]

Arnold Bittlinger, a Lutheran theologian, spells this thought out in somewhat greater detail: "While baptism is an event which occurs at a particular moment in a person's life, both Catholic and Protestant tradition recognize that the efficacy of baptism is not tied to the moment of time wherein it is administered. What is given in baptism may become active or realized at other moments in the life of the believer." [48]

In baptism one is given all the things (e.g., gifts, ministries, workings, services, etc.) that he will ever receive in Christ—potentially. "But if that baptism is not actualized in the life of the baptized, God's purpose in baptism has failed of achievement. It would have been better if the person had not been baptized at all. The potential given in baptism must be appropriated in the personal experience of the individual." [49]

There is no thought here of baptism functioning in some kind of magical or automatic sense. Rather, baptism functions as a central factor in the initiation of a relationship. The potential of the Christian life is the potential of that relationship, just as the potential of a marriage is the potential of the relationship which can develop between husband and wife. When one is joined to Christ, baptized into His Body, he has entered into a relationship which has the potential to unfold and develop in many ways.[50]

One way in which this relationship may be expressed is through a signal breakthrough or release of the power of the Holy Spirit.

This is one way of describing or understanding the kind of experience which multitudes of people are experiencing in our day. It is a release, or actualization, of a potential which exists in one's relationship with Christ.[51] Charismatics would see here a parallel to an experience of "awakening," in which a baptized person at a later time comes to a vivid awareness of the forgiving grace of Christ.

At this point we see a distinction between the Lutheran and the classical Pentecostal way of describing the bestowal and manifestation of the Holy Spirit. The Lutheran sees it as a releasing of the Spirit which has already been given, for power and ministry. The "spring of water" (John 4:14) becomes an "outflowing river" (John 7:38). Classical Pentecostalism sees it as an added endowment of the Spirit. The Spirit comes upon the believer, enduing him with power. Both speak of the same essential reality, one theologically, the other experientially.

In speaking of the coming of the Spirit, Jesus used both the imagery of "outflowing" (John 7:38) and the imagery of "coming upon" (Acts 1:8). And in both cases it is directed toward believers. Each image portrays an aspect of the truth. The imagery of "outflowing" recognizes the already existing relationship between the Spirit and the believer. The imagery of "coming upon" describes the experience of the Spirit coming into one's life in a fresh way.

The term "baptism with the Holy Spirit" presents some problems in a Lutheran context. Like the term "charismatic," it has a twofold meaning. In one sense every Christian has been "baptized with the Spirit" inasmuch as he has received Christian baptism in the name of the Father, Son, and Holy Spirit. In this sense baptism with the Holy Spirit belongs to the inheritance of every Christian.

The term, however, is also used in an experiential sense. When used in this way it refers to the event or process by which the power of the Holy Spirit is released in a fresh way. In this sense baptism with the Holy Spirit is the Spirit being actualized, or coming to more conscious manifestation, in one's life.

In the charismatic renewal the term "baptism with the Holy Spirit" is used almost exclusively in this second, or experiential sense. This usage is legitimate, for the church had not made much use of this term in its theological sense; other terms were used to describe the basic reality of becoming a Christian. Until the Holiness-Pentecostal movement broke on the scene, "baptism with the Holy Spirit" was a largely unemployed term. It had no established cluster of meanings attached to it, so it was available for use in this specialized, experiential sense.

The word "baptism" carries with it the connotation of an initial or initiating experience. For many people, charismatic renewal has had that character: What they may have known theoretically, they have now been initiated into experientially. Thus *"baptism with the Holy Spirit"* is an appropriate term to describe their experience.

The experiential use of the term is also biblical. In Acts, Luke uses a variety of terms to describe manifest demonstrations of the Holy Spirit; to be baptized with the Holy Spirit is one of them. In 10:44-11:18, for instance, five different terms are used to refer to the same event: the Holy Spirit (1) *fell* on all who heard. . . . The (2) *gift* of the Holy Spirit was (3) *poured out.* . . . They (4) *received* the Holy Spirit. . . . They were (5) *baptized with* the Holy Spirit. Here, as throughout Acts, Luke presents the working of the Holy Spirit in terms of manifest experience. The person who describes his charismatic experience as a "baptism with the Spirit" is using the term in a Lukan sense.

The same would be true if one said, "The Spirit came on me," or, "I was filled with the Spirit." Luke uses all these terms more-or-less synonymously. In the charismatic renewal usage has tended to narrow down to the one term, "baptism with the Holy Spirit." This may represent an unnecessary impoverishment of expression. Those involved in the renewal might well consider the example of Acts, and employ a greater variety of terms to describe their experience of the Holy Spirit, even expanding Luke's vocabulary with terms such as "release of the Spirit," "awakening to the Spirit," "fullness of the Spirit," "renewal of the Spirit," etc.

Classical Pentecostalism generally taught[52] that the initial physical evidence that one had been baptized with the Holy Spirit was that he spoke in tongues. The charismatic movement has somewhat muted this doctrine of "initial evidence." [53] The occurrence of tongues, however, is widespread. It is a usual experience for one participating in the charismatic renewal. The significance and value of this particular gift is considered more extensively in chapter nine.

CHAPTER SEVEN

Baptism

Historically, charismatic renewal does not seem to be tied to any particular theology of baptism. The Montanists (2nd century), Jansenists (18th century), and Irvingites (19th century) appear to have followed current baptismal practice. While there were some Baptists active in the Irvingite movement, they were not as influential as those from Anglican or Presbyterian backgrounds. The Catholic Apostolic Church, which developed out of this renewal, adopted a sacramental view of baptism, and practiced the baptism of infants.

The main stream of classical Pentecostalism introduced no innovation in the theology or practice of baptism.[54] They adopted a Baptist view, which was predominant in that part of the American religious culture from which they sprang. In Germany, some Pentecostal groups retained an essentially Lutheran view of baptism.

The impact of charismatic renewal does not seem to have any intrinsic effect upon one's theology and practice of baptism. The tendency, rather, is to continue one's normal baptismal practice, perhaps with a heightened sense of appreciation, as was the case with the Catholic Apostolic Church.

Where questions about baptism have come up in the charismatic movement, it has been due not to charismatic experience, as such, but to the ecumenical nature of the movement. People from different theological traditions have come into meaningful encounter with one another. Old questions and differences about baptism have come in for fresh examination.

In the early years of the charismatic movement, Lutherans had considerable exposure to classical Pentecostal theology. Because they had come to identify in a deep and meaningful way with Pentecostal experience, some, quite uncritically, took on certain features of Pentecostal theology, including baptismal theology. They questioned the validity of their baptism as infants. Some were rebaptized, by immersion. This did not come as an outgrowth of the charismatic experience itself, but as a result of the general influence of Pentecostal theology in those first years. By the end of the 1960s, as Roman Catholic, Lutheran, and Anglican influence increased, this trend began to subside.

Questions about Lutheran baptismal practice, however, still circulate through the renewal. What about infant baptism? What about immersion baptism? What about rebaptism?

These are questions I can identify with. I had to face them in a very personal way in the early days of the movement.

About the same time I experienced the baptism with the Holy Spirit, I read a book which a seminary classmate had recommended to me: *The Teaching of the Church Regarding Baptism* by Karl Barth. It shook me up.

Karl Barth is a persuasive arguer. And in this little book he argues against the practice of infant baptism. It forced me to think deeply about a practice

which I had never before seriously questioned.
Though I continued to baptize children, according
to the practice of our church, I felt increasingly uneasy doing so.

A few months later, another "baptism question"
landed in my lap. Several friends confided to me
that they had been rebaptized by immersion. After
having experienced the baptism with the Holy Spirit,
they had come to question their baptism as infants.

"I was only sprinkled as a baby. And I didn't
even know what was happening. But *this*—this was
my own decision."

Only later did I come to recognize the subtle danger imbedded in that phrase, "my own decision."
At the time, the testimony of these friends served
to increase my uncertainty about our whole practice
of baptism.

Was this God's way of speaking to me? Was He
using my study of the subject, and now personal
testimonies from sincere Christians, to call into question a long-standing practice of the church? Was
He, in fact, telling *me* to be rebaptized?

The answer did not come all at once. It unfolded
slowly, over a period of time. But the essence of
it broke in on me in one unsuspecting moment.

I had been asked to give a lecture at an ecumenical
conference in Germany. The theme of the conference was, "One Lord, One Faith, One Baptism." In
preparing my lecture, I came across a book by
a 19th-century German theologian. In his discussion
of baptism, one particular phrase caught my attention: "The question whether infants may be baptized
can naturally be decided by God alone." [56]

It was so simple, so unpretentious. Here I had
been struggling to decide something which was already decided. The primary question was not whether infants can believe, or whether faith must pre-

cede baptism, or whether baptism in water is also baptism with the Spirit, or anything else. The primary question, the only question that really counts, is *what has God decided*? And in that moment a quiet conviction quickened within me that He would show me what He had decided.

What About Baptism?

Karl Barth's criticism of infant baptism arose in view of a particular setting: The state churches of Europe, where virtually every child born is baptized as a matter of custom. The majority of parents have no practical involvement in the life of the Christian community. Less that 5% even attend worship services, yet 95% bring their children to be baptized. In America, the percentages are somewhat more encouraging, but still well below the standard of the early church, where it was well understood that children who were baptized would grow up within the sphere of the church.[57]

When we see this kind of abuse of baptism, it is quite natural to conclude that people put altogether too much faith in baptism. But actually, the reverse is the case. They put too *little* faith in baptism. They do not reckon seriously upon what God does in baptism. Karl Boehm, a 19th-century German theologian, wrote, "If faith in the act of God performed in baptism were a living thing in the clergy and in the churches of this day, the preaching of the former and the Christian life of the latter would assume another form." [58] The first conviction that needs to grip our hearts is that God acts decisively in baptism.

Baptism and Salvation

Baptism is tied to the forgiveness of sins. "Repent,

and *be baptized* every one of you in the name of Jesus Christ *for the forgiveness of sins*" (Acts 2:38). The Greek text suggests movement: Baptism is the vehicle which moves a person into the forgiveness of sins.

Baptism rescues from judgment. "In the days of Noah . . . a few . . . were saved through water. *Baptism*, which corresponds to this, *now saves you*" (1 Pet. 3:20-21). The deliverance of Israel through the Red Sea is likewise seen as a parallel to baptism. The children of Israel were "baptized into Moses . . . in the Sea" (1 Cor. 10:2). Through this 'baptism,' they were delivered from Pharaoh's power. The typology is evident: Through the waters of baptism, we are delivered from spiritual slavery; we are no longer under the authority of sin and Satan.

Salvation is thus clearly linked to baptism. "He who believes and is baptized will be saved" (Mark 16:16). Most Bible scholars understand Titus 3:5 as a reference to baptism also: "He saved us . . . by the *washing of regeneration*."

While baptism may be the occasion for a public testimony of one's faith, this is a secondary factor. The primary emphasis of Scripture is upon what *God* does in baptism. He uses baptism as a means to help accomplish His saving work.

Baptism Unites Us with Christ

How is a believer united with Christ? By what means does God graft us as members into His Body? According to Scripture, God has chosen to accomplish this miracle by means of *baptism*.

Lutheran theologian James Kallas points out that there is not one sentence, in all the writings of St. Paul, where union with Christ is effected apart from baptism. "The place where the Christian is joined to Christ, or comes to be in Christ, is not the moment of faith at all—but it is the moment of baptism. That is why Paul has such a powerful view of baptism, for it is that act which joins a man to Jesus." [59]

Certainly faith is involved in the process, but that faith does not function apart from baptism. "As many of you as were baptized into Christ have put on Christ" (Gal. 3:27).

Faith may prepare a person for union with Christ, baptism seals it. In order to come out of slavery, the children of Israel had to put their faith in Moses (who is a type of Christ).[60] They had to believe him, and follow him—follow him *into the Red Sea.* Their faith was specifically a faith *unto 'baptism.'* We might say, quite accurately, that they were "saved by faith." But we would understand that to mean that by faith they followed Moses through the saving waters of the Red Sea.

Baptism Unites Us with Other Christians

We are not made members of the Body of Christ on the basis of a common "experience," or a doctrine, or a standard of holiness, or membership in a particular denomination, or on any other basis that men might devise. "By one Spirit we were all *baptized* into one body" (1 Cor. 12:13). The one objective sign uniting all Christians is the name of Christ which has been placed upon them in baptism.

That the practice of baptism has been terribly abused must be evident even to an on-looking pagan. That multitudes of baptized people show no evidence of God's work in their lives is, for the church, a shame and humiliation. But our failure to use properly a God-given ordinance does not license us to substitute one of our own in its place.

Every attempt to establish some other basis for fellowship in the Christian Church has resulted only

in division. We will not heal the divisions in the
Body of Christ by seeking after some other basis
for unity than that which God has ordained. Our
unity is not through an 'experience' of Christ, nor
through adherence to a commandment of Christ, nor
through a correct belief about Christ, but our unity
is through *common membership in His Body,* which,
according to Scripture, God effects through baptism.

To acknowledge what God has done in baptism
is nothing other than to acknowledge what God has
done in the death and resurrection of Christ, and
this in a most personal way. For baptism is the means
God has chosen to channel the saving work of Christ
into a person's life. "All of us who have been baptized
into Christ Jesus were baptized into his death. We
were buried therefore with him *by baptism* into
death, so that as Christ was raised from the dead
by the glory of the Father, we too might walk in
newness of life" (Rom. 6:3-4). To believe in the
power of baptism is to believe in the God who, in
sovereign wisdom, chose it as His means of uniting
people with His Son and with one another. "To
firmly believe this," said Martin Luther, "must make
the heart happy and cause one to love and praise
God." [61]

What About Infant Baptism?

We noted that the primary question in regard to
infant baptism is simply this: "What has God decided?" If God has decided against it, any attempt
to initiate it would be presumptuous. If God has decided in favor of it, any argument against it would
be foolish.

Our first door of inquiry, of course, would be the
Scripture. But here we encounter a difficulty. We
are like a student who comes to the house of one

of his professors to ask a question, only to discover that the professor is "not available." When it comes to the question of infant baptism, clear scriptural evidence simply is not available.

Edmund Schlink, professor of theology at Heidelberg, in his exhaustive study of the subject concludes, "On the basis of the New Testament, infant baptism can neither be excluded nor proved." [62] In the New Testament, most of the recorded baptisms are clearly adult baptisms. But this is what one would expect in any report of a first-generation missionary church. We would encounter the same thing in the report of a Lutheran missionary society, moving for the first time into a pagan culture.

The fact that infant baptism is not specifically mentioned in the New Testament proves nothing. It simply underlines the fact that conclusive New Testament evidence on this question is not available. On the one hand, there is no clear case where an infant is baptized. On the other hand, there is no case where we see the child of Christian parents coming for baptism at a later age. Nor does the New Testament give any example of a "dedication rite" for Christian infants. The New Testament simply does not answer this question.

If one finds that his professor is "not available," one might pose his question to the professor's wife, or colleague; perhaps they have heard the professor discuss this particular question, and could give pretty much the same kind of answer that the professor himself would give.

Who would be in the best position to know what Jesus' intention was in regard to the baptism of children? To whom would He most likely have revealed himself in this matter? The answer, of course, is His *apostles*. The New Testament records only a fraction of the teaching and instruction which Jesus imparted to them. (See John 20:30; 21:25; Acts 1:3.) It is not unlikely that He gave them specific instructions on this matter. Or, the Holy Spirit may have revealed to them how they were to handle this question, as He did in many other regards. If we can find out what the apostles did, we will come as close as possible to getting a direct, authoritative answer to our basic question. "What has *God* decided?"

This points us to our necessary area of inquiry, which is *the evidence of church history.* "The problem of infant baptism," says British scholar George Every, "is first of all an historical problem, not an exegetical or theological one." [63] Do we find, in the early records of the church, any evidence of how the apostles handled the question of infant baptism?

"History," says one student of the subject, "is a friend of infant baptism. Its opponents are not justified in casting off the position as a spiritual aberration. A view so widespread in the church is not just the result of medieval fancy. One finds its origins deep in the roots of church history." [64]

The church order of Hippolytus, which originated in Rome about 215 A.D., contains the directive, "First the little ones should be baptized. All who can speak for themselves should speak. For those however who cannot, their parents or another who belongs to their family should speak." [65]

Origen, writing around 240 A.D., said, "The church received a tradition from the Apostles to give baptism to infants too." [66]

Nowhere in the records of the church do we find the counter-argument, that infant baptism was an innovation. Says Karl Boehm: "Considering the conscientiousness and severity with which the bishops of the first centuries resisted every innovation and change from the apostolic practice, and that they allowed authority to nothing save that which came down to them from the Apostles, it must have been impossible in so important a matter as baptism, that so great an innovation as that of infant baptism (were it an innovation) could have been universally introduced without much contention and opposition." [67]

The rejection of infant baptism as a matter of principle first arose in the 16th century *as a result of a new understanding of the individual person.*[68] This fact is of utmost importance. The challenge to infant baptism did not arise from a fresh study of Scripture, nor from a new discovery of apostolic practice, but from a new *secular understanding of the nature of man.* "Belief" was seen in rationalistic and volitional terms, an act of the mind and the will. "Because an infant cannot think or decide, it cannot have faith, and therefore it should not be baptized." To this day, that is the only argument raised against the validity of infant baptism. One tosses off the sentence as though it were self-evident truth: "A child can't believe." But that 'truth,' upon examination, is neither self-evident, nor is it biblical.

The Bible does not see faith merely in rationalistic terms, but in *relational* terms. Faith is a relationship of love and trust between God and man. The Bible does not limit this relationship to those who are able to express it verbally.

"Thou art He who didst bring me forth from the womb; Thou didst make me *trust* when upon my mother's breasts" (Ps. 22:9, NASB). Here the quality of faith is ascribed to a nursing infant. Jesus referred to a little child whom He held in His arms as "this little one *who believes in me*" (Mark 9:42). Far from denying to children the capability of faith, Jesus holds them up as an example for adults. "Whoever does not receive the kingdom of God like a child shall not enter it" (Luke 18:17). God's problem is not with infants who cannot believe, but with adults who insist on doubting.

A person may look back upon his baptism as an infant and say, "I didn't know what I was doing ... nothing happened." But that is a statement which is incapable of being proved. You cannot *remember* what you did, but that does not mean that you did nothing. You have no way of knowing (intellectually) how your *spirit* was responding to God at your baptism. Nor can you say "nothing happened" simply because you have no recollection of the event. That would be like an Israelite child who had been carried as an infant through the Red Sea on his mother's lap, sound asleep, in later years saying, "Nothing happened."

Our understanding of "what happened" cannot hang on the slender thread of our own recollection. What happened in your baptism depends upon what God did, not what you remember. "You were buried with him in baptism, in which you were also raised with him, *through faith in the working of God.*"

Faith is a gift of God (Col. 2:12). Neither adult nor child can believe unless God gives the gift. And He is able to give it to an infant as well as to an adult. The fact that an infant cannot respond to this gift verbally does not mean that he cannot receive it.

The notion that children cannot believe is rooted in a nonbiblical anthropology. The Bible, as we have noted above, gives ample evidence that even tiny babies can respond to God in faith. John the Baptist leaped for joy, at the presence of the Lord, when he was still in his mother's womb! (Luke 1:44).

A chilling documentation of children's openness to the spiritual world is the evidence that children raised in homes where witchcraft is practiced can come into spiritual bondage from their earliest years.

If Satan can gain access to a child's inner life, surely the Holy Spirit can. And is not this one reason that the church for so many centuries has baptized its infants—to rescue them from the dominion of Satan when they are too little to help themselves? The most ancient liturgies of baptism lay special stress on this point; the child is "snatched from Satan's clutches" into the protective bosom of the church.

At an ecumenical conference on baptism, in Germany, a theologian of the Eastern Orthodox Church described this particular aspect of baptism, as it occurs in the baptismal liturgy of his church. The child is delivered into the arms of the priest, at which point the parents turn and "spit on the devil." At another point there is a threefold exorcism, whereby the child is delivered from the power and authority of Satan. The central emphasis of the baptismal service is upon the victory of Christ over the powers of darkness, the deliverance and rescue of the child into the company of God's people.

After the lecture, a Baptist minister said, "Now *there* is a case for infant baptism!"

A generation ago such goings-on would have been dismissed by some as a quaint carry-over from an age of superstition. Today, with the upsurge of the occult, people are coming to recognize that the power of evil is no mere superstition; when St. Paul said that we wrestle against spiritual hosts of wickedness (see Eph. 6:12), he was describing an awesome reality—a reality that can affect the lives of children as well as adults.

And this, in turn, points up the essential problem in regard to infant baptism: *pastoral care.* Let it be said here that we make no case for an indiscriminate practice of infant baptism. In our congregation, no child is baptized unless his parents are *active members of the congregation.* Jesus' command to disciple all nations unto Him contains a twofold instruction: *baptize* and *teach* (Matt. 28: 19-20). Unless we have reasonable assurance that the child will be brought up in the Christian faith, we cannot responsibly baptize him.

But where a child's spiritual nurture is provided for, then we see no hindrance to that child's full incorporation into the Body of Christ through baptism.

What About Immersion Baptism?

The Roman Catholic Church, in its new rite for the baptism of infants, has adopted the practice of immersion. This could set a precedent for its inclusion in the new rite of adult baptism.[69]

The Eastern Orthodox Church has always followed the practice of infant immersion.

Martin Luther wrote, "The Greek for baptize means to dip something entirely in water. Without doubt the German word *Taufe* (baptism) is derived from the word *tief* (deep), so that one sinks deeply into the water ... therefore one should do justice to the signification of baptism and give a sign that is full and complete." [70]

Surely the symbolism of death-and-resurrection is more vivid when one is totally immersed than when water is poured over the head. It could be deeply meaningful to restore this practice to the churches which do not now practice it.

This does not mean that other modes of baptism are invalid. The word in Greek admits to various shades of meaning. (In Mark 7:4 and in Luke 11:38 it is properly translated "wash.") The apostolic church recognized that situations might arise where there simply was not enough water for an immersion baptism. In the *Didache*, one of the earliest writings after the New Testament, instructions for nonimmersion baptism are given.

Nevertheless, in seeking to enrich its worship and

sacramental life, the church today could well look to a reviving of the ancient and meaningful practice of immersion.

What About Rebaptism?

The simplest thing to say about rebaptism is that it is impossible. Baptism is not baptism unless God does something. In baptism, the Holy Spirit grafts us into the Body of Christ (1 Cor. 12:13). But He does this once, not over and over again. He does not ungraft us, then regraft us into Christ anytime we decide to go through the baptismal service. If God graciously acted in our (original) baptism, then that is the baptism He recognizes. We cannot twist His arm to baptize us again. A subtle element of self-will can be at work when one goes through a baptismal service that is "my own decision." The prior question needs to be considered: "What decision has God made in this regard?"

"Rebaptism" may be the occasion for a personal appropriation or experiencing of the benefits of baptism, or a rededication to one's baptism vows. It is not, however, New Testament baptism. Either one is baptized or one is not. There is no halfway house.

We have seen people seek rebaptism for the very best motives: the desire to be completely identified with the Lord and obedient to Him. That desire, however, can be fulfilled in another way; less dramatic, perhaps, but nevertheless real.

When I was wrestling with this question myself, I one day knelt down and simply *thanked God for what He had done for me in baptism.* I reaffirmed the reality of that act. I rededicated myself to its vows of faith and holiness. It was a quiet moment, but one which I have never forgotten. Baptism is a one-time event, but by faith it may be continually renewed.

CHAPTER EIGHT

Understanding Spiritual Experience

A right understanding of "spiritual experience" has become something of a problem when used in a Christian context. The reason for this is that we have tended to narrow its meaning down to some of the emotional or psychological aspects of spiritual experience. When we talk about "spiritual experience" we concern ourselves mainly with what the person feels or thinks. This approach, or course, is highly individualistic, for no two people will have the same reaction to the same event. Therefore it has been easy to dismiss spiritual experience as a purely personal matter.

Luther understood experience in a more profound way. Salvation is an experienced event. Apart from experience Christianity is mere history, mere theory, empty words. A Christian, by definition, is someone who has experienced an encounter with the living God.

Of course spiritual experience will have its emotional and psychological aspects (as if it were possible to talk of an encounter with God devoid of all feeling or thought!). But behind the experience lies something awesomely objective: An encounter with the living God. And the primary question is not, "How do I feel or think during or after such an encounter?" This is important but it is not primary. The primary question is, "What does God have in mind when He initiates such encounters?"

Behind this question lies an assumption, of course; namely that there *is* a God, and that He *does* initiate encounters with people. This belief was fundamental to Luther's whole understanding of the Holy Spirit.[71] It is a foundational axiom of the historic Christian faith (see Heb. 11:6). Article 20 of the Augsburg Confession clearly recognizes the experiential dimension of justification: "Although this teaching [of justification by faith] is despised by inexperienced men, God-fearing and anxious consciences find *by experience* that it offers the greatest consolation because the consciences of men cannot be pacified by any work but only by faith when they are sure that for Christ's sake they have a gracious God." [72]

Our basic attitude toward spiritual experience will have a determinative affect upon the way we understand the charismatic renewal. If we basically discount the significance of spiritual experience, we will tend to focus upon the psychological and emotional states which accompany charismatic experience. The Presbyterian study of the charismatic movement sees a particular danger at this point—

It will be a dark and tragic day in the life of Christianity if psychological norms are to become the criteria by which the truth or the untruth of religious experience is judged. Psychological insight has enriched, deepened, and humbled our knowledge of ourselves beyond measure; but, when it is asked for a decisive answer to the question of whether a man has or has not experienced the living Christ it is an aborted and inappropriate use of the science.[73]

If, on the other hand, we affirm the reality and

significance of spiritual experience, we will concern ourselves not only with human reactions, but with the reality and purpose of God which lie behind and give rise to the experiences.

In attempting to understand the experience of charismatics, it may be helpful to draw attention to certain features of their experience which may be unfamiliar to some Lutherans.

1. *'Crisis' as contrasted with 'growth.'* Lutherans have generally understood the Christian life in terms of gradual growth and development. We have been less familiar with the peak or crisis-type experience, [74] though this is not absent from our tradition. The charismatic renewal has brought this second mode of Christian experience to the fore. While some in the renewal may experience a release of the Spirit as a process of gradual unfolding, it is more usually experienced as a specific event.

These two modes of Christian experience are not contradictory to one another, but complementary. They are different ways in which one's relationship to Christ may develop.

In any relationship, there will be times of quiet growth, and moments of more dramatic breakthrough. The balance between these two modes of development will vary from individual to individual. Also, the times in which one lives will to some extent affect the interplay of the 'growth' and 'breakthrough' motifs. In wartime large numbers of young men move into sober, responsible adulthood by means of crisis; in quiet times, many would tend to mature somewhat more gradually. Similarly, in times of spiritual ferment or transition, crisis-type experiences are more likely to be widespread.

For a time, to begin with, a breakthrough experience may separate a person from his roots. He is caught up in the exploration of a new dimension of life. One thinks of young people who fall in love and all but lose contact with the world around them.

But if a breakthrough experience is to contribute something of value to life, it must establish itself in relation to the basic foundations of the life from which it sprang. The young lovers, as Dietrich Bonhoeffer has said, begin by seeing only themselves in the world. In marriage, they must go on to see themselves as a link in the chain of generations, which God causes to come and to pass away to His glory, and which He calls into His kingdom.[75]

Those who have experienced a renewal in the Holy Spirit will find the blessing further deepened when they recognize it as a means of continuing and strengthening that life into which they have already been initiated by water and the Word.

2. *'Personal' as contrasted with 'corporate.'* It is sometimes tossed off as a truism that the charismatic renewal is a hotbed of hysterical emotionalism. This may result from mistakenly equating the personal with the emotional. Kilian McDonnell, in his extensive firsthand research of the movement, noted this tendency in his own initial reactions—

> When I first attended charismatic prayer meetings, I said they were "emotional." I felt somewhat uncomfortable in them, I told myself, because I was not a particularly emotional person. But as I continued to go, I came to realize that the emotional level, as such, was not significantly different from a normal Catholic worship service. What was different was the *personal* element: the people spoke of their relationship with God in a highly personal way. This was strange to me, and that is what made me at first feel uncomfortable.[76]

Many Lutherans would echo McDonnell's sentiments. They are more at home with corporate and formal expressions of their faith. The spontaneous, personal idiom which they meet in charismatic prayer meetings makes them feel uncomfortable.

On the other hand, this personal dimension can bring a fresh vitality to the reality of the faith relationship. This is especially true in the area of worship.

> It is of ultimate significance that we understand Christianity not as our possession of religious truths but as the Lord's possession of us, and that we stand before him in a direct faith relationship. We have not always been aware of the subtle shift in our attention from God's person to the church's doctrine.
>
> The easy, uninhibited style of worship observed in neo-Pentecostalism offers a constructive opportunity to review both the content and method of staid liturgical forms. In the Reformation tradition, the style of worship has never been canonized, and we would plead for toleration as persons worship more freely.[77]

3. *Emotion as contrasted with intellect.* An intellectual response to the faith has generally come easier to Lutherans than an emotional response. This has given to Lutheranism a stability which charismatics should not lightly pass off. On the other hand, a wholesome emotional response can enrich and deepen one's encounter with God. God does not encounter us merely at the level of our minds. He engages our whole humanity.

It is well to recognize at this point that an intellectual response to the gospel is just as much an "experience" as an emotional or volitional response. The theologian who sits quietly in his study, studying the Scriptures, or laying out a systematic presentation of Christian doctrine, is *experiencing* the faith just as surely as the charismatic who prays fervently in a prayer meeting.

The two experiences are different in that one may

engage primarily the intellect, the other primarily the imagination or feelings. But it is altogether inaccurate to say that the charismatic is involved with experience, while the theologian is involved with, well, something else, though that something else is never precisely defined. Indeed, if we were to examine the situations more closely, we would probably discover that the theologizing involves no little feeling, and the prayer some considerable powers of thought.

It is a false dichotomy to pit experience against scholarship. Scholarly work involves one in particular kinds of experiences.

Nor is faith to be contrasted with experience. Faith is inseparable from the experience of the one in whom it takes root. The person who boasts that he lives by faith, not by experience, misunderstands the nature of faith. To live by faith inevitably involves a person in experience. It may be the experience of quiet, inward trusting; of stormy repentance; of joyful singing; of patient reflection; of rigorous scholarship. Faith gives rise to the broadest possible spectrum of experience, for it leaves no aspect of our life untouched by the transforming presence of Christ.

What we are actually talking about is *varieties* of experience. Differing kinds of experience not only enrich life, they also serve as healthy correctives to one another. Every strength is a potential weakness if carried to an extreme. The spontaneous charismatic needs the counterpoise of the careful theologian. Spontaneity without scholarship can lead to superficiality or fanaticism. Likewise, the theologian needs the counterpoise of those who have experienced the faith in more direct, intuitive ways. In his study of Martin Luther, Roland Bainton said, "Luther verged on saying that emotional sensitivity is a mode of revelation. Those who are predisposed to fall into despondency as well as to rise into ecstasy may be able to view reality from an angle different from that of ordinary folk. Yet it is a true angle; and when the problem or the religious object has been once so viewed, others less sensitive will be able to look from a new vantage point and testify that the insight is valid." [78]

Within the Body of Christ there needs to be a wholesome interaction between people with differing kinds of experience. It's easy to get caught up in one's own little circle, whereby one becomes impoverished and un-self-critical. Theologians and charismatics alike can fall into the trap of going along with what is fashionable in their particular circles. The "assured results of scientific scholarship" and the "leading of the Lord" are meant to augment, enrich, and, where necessary, correct one another.

The church can be thankful that a charismatic renewal has arisen as a source of correction to its theological task. Likewise, the charismatic renewal can be thankful when its experience of spiritual gifts is measured against the theological standard of the church.

4. *Fellowship as contrasted with individualism.* The kind of fellowship one encounters in the charismatic renewal can prove uncomfortable for some Lutherans. It is generally warm, spontaneous, and demonstrative. People often embrace when they meet one another. They speak freely and eagerly about spiritual things. They pray readily with and for one another. In some sectors of the renewal more intensive forms of Christian fellowship are emerging, including various kinds of communities, and relationships involving a high degree of commitment and interdependence.

Where one's religious life-style tends toward formality, and his personal life-style toward individualism, some of these expressions of fellowship can pose a threat. Charismatics, however, would say that Scripture calls us to a more intensive kind of fellowship than is generally experienced in the church today.

The charismatic renewal has a positive contribution to make to the life of the church. Many charismatics demonstrate a commendable zeal in prayer, Bible study, personal witnessing, stewardship, and social concern.[79] Their experience of the Holy Spirit has led to a deepening of their commitment to Christ.

Likewise the church has a contribution to make to the charismatic renewal. Part of the renewing work of the Holy Spirit is to refresh those things that are already part of our tradition—our heritage of worship, hymnody, theology. While we may benefit from interaction with other traditions, we should not uncritically import their religious culture into a Lutheran setting. To do so could result in a kind of impoverishment.[80] In one of his first contacts with charismatic renewal in the Lutheran church, David du Plessis [81] said, "Don't copy the Pentecostals. What they have is fine for them, but it won't work in a Lutheran setting. Let the Holy Spirit bring forth among Lutherans what He wants to, what fits your background and culture." [82]

CHAPTER NINE

Spiritual Gifts

"The purpose of the charismatic renewal is fullness of life in the Holy Spirit, the exercise in the church of the gifts of the Holy Spirit, directed toward the proclamation that Jesus is Lord to the Glory of the Father." [83]

It is in the context of this purpose that we must understand the emphasis on spiritual gifts which we find in the charismatic renewal. Spiritual gifts (*charismata*) are concrete manifestations of the Holy Spirit whom the believers have received. The manifestation of these gifts exemplify and authenticate the church's proclamation that Jesus is Lord, bringing glory to the Father.

The spectrum of spiritual gifts mentioned in Scripture is broad and varied—from the gift of eternal life (Rom. 6:23), to the gift of celibacy (1 Cor. 7:7). Alongside the more unusual gifts such as healing, miracles, and speaking in tongues (1 Cor. 12:9-10), we find the seemingly more ordinary gifts of administration, helping, giving, and teaching (1 Cor. 12:28; Rom. 12:7-8). And there is no indication that the list of gifts in the New Testament is exhaustive.[84] The ways in which the Holy Spirit may manifest himself are varied and many.

The charismatic renewal has emphasized some gifts more than others, notably the catalogue given in 1 Corinthians 12:8-10. Charismatics need to be on guard lest this emphasis become a permanent stance. To begin with, however, it has served a useful purpose by calling the church's attention to some of the more neglected spiritual gifts. Kilian McDonnell illustrates this in the following way:

> There are differences between a community of Christians in the early Church and a community of Christians in the contemporary Church. In the first place, this difference is to be found in a difference of awareness, expectation, and openness. By the way of example, imagine for the moment that the full spectrum of how the Spirit comes to visibility in a charism extends from A to Z.
>
> It is here supposed that in the section of the spectrum which extends from A to P are such charisms as generosity in giving alms and other acts of mercy (Rom. 12:8) and teaching activities of various kinds. The section of the spectrum which extends from P to Z is supposed here to include such charisms as prophecy, gifts of healing, working of miracles, tongues, interpretation.
>
> It is evident that in the life of the early Church the communities expected that the Spirit would manifest himself in ministries and services which might fall within the spectrum which extends from A to P, but they also expected the Spirit to manifest himself in other ministries and services within the section of the spectrum which extends from P to Z. They were aware that prophecy, gifts of healing, working of miracles, tongues, and interpretation were real charisms, real possibilities for the life of the Church. The early Christian communities were aware that these gifts were gifts to the Church, they expected that they would be manifested in their communities, they were open to them, and these gifts were in fact operative among them. In

this they differ from most contemporary communities. Communities in the Church today are not aware
that the charisms in the section of the spectrum
which extends from P to Z are possibilities for the
life of the Church. These communities do not expect the charisms in this section to be operative
and manifest in their midst. To that degree they
are not really open to them, and in most communities these charisms are, as a matter of fact, not
operative.

For a community to have a limited expectation
as to how the Spirit will manifest himself in its midst
can profoundly affect the life and experience of that
community. It can affect its public eucharistic
worship, the private prayer of its members, the manner in which it proclaims the Gospel and serves the
world. And if a community limits how the Spirit
manifests himself there is some measure of impoverishment in the total life of that local church.[85]

How does the church feel about its members who
manifest spiritual gifts, particularly those gifts in
the P-Z end of the spectrum? In considerable measure this has been an embarrassment to the church.

Prophesying, praying in tongues, interpreting,
healing, are not ways of behavior which the mores
of our culture expect from mature, responsible
adults. Persons who act in these ways deviate from
the expected behavior patterns and are therefore
accepted in normal social contacts only with some
embarrassment.

One could rightly ask whether social accept-
ability is a proper behavioral norm for a Christian.
The Gospel proclaims truths and norms of behavior
which are not socially acceptable. The question is
asked: How does a Christian judge behavior? Do
the mores of society fully determine morality for a
Christian? [86]

How *does* the church judge the behavior of its

people? Is it captive to the mores of society which happen to be in vogue at the present time? Instead of being embarrassed, ought not the church be grateful that these treasures of the Spirit are again active in our midst?

Speaking in Tongues[87]

One gift, more than any other, has come to be identified with the charismatic renewal—speaking in tongues. Because it has been so much the subject of discussion, and so often misunderstood, it merits special consideration.

Speaking in tongues presents us with something of an anomaly. On the one hand, tongues appears to play a significant role in terms of the dynamism and growth of a movement. Without the emphasis on tongues it is doubtful that there would have been either a Pentecostal or a charismatic movement.[88] On the other hand, tongues is not the primary focus of attention in charismatic circles. Kilian McDonnell has correctly observed that charismatics "show a little impatience with the outsider's preoccupation with tongues, which they consider peripheral. For them the issue is not tongues, but fullness of life in the Spirit." [89]

The charismatic movement cannot be reduced simply to speaking in tongues. Yet neither can it be understood or explained apart from tongues. To grasp the significance of this "least of the gifts" is not the least of our challenge in trying to understand the charismatic renewal. Paul Tournier, in his book, *The Meaning of Persons,* says, "Speaking in tongues appears to answer to the need of the spirit to *express the inexpressible,* to carry the dialogue with God beyond the narrow limits of clearly intelligible language."

Charismatics may not talk about speaking in

tongues at any great length unless they are questioned about it. In one sense, they regard it as a minor aspect of their renewal in the Spirit. Those outside the renewal, however, need to realize that this does not mean that charismatics regard the gift lightly.

Those who have experienced this manifestation of the Spirit find that it has great blessing and value. It is no 'frill' or 'extra' in their Christian life—something which they could now take or leave depending upon their mood. It has sparked a deep, often a transforming change in their spiritual life. One man expressed it this way: "Speaking in tongues was a spiritual breakthrough for me."

One speaks in tongues, for the most part, in his private devotions. *This is by far its most important use and value.* If offers the believer a new dimension in prayer. Although one does not know what he is saying as he speaks in tongues, he does have a clear sense that he is praying to God. The heightened awareness of God's presence is one of the greatest blessings one receives through this experience. A seventy-year-old pastor who came into this experience said, "Christ has never before been so real to me!"

The Value of Speaking in Tongues

Speaking in tongues brings to one's private devotions the special blessing of "praying in the spirit" as distinct from praying with the understanding. This comes out in 1 Corinthians 14:2, 14, and 28: "One who speaks in a tongue speaks not to men but to God.... If I pray in a tongue, my spirit prays but my mind is unfruitful.... If there is no one to interpret, let each of them keep silence in church and speak to himself and to God."

One immediately wonders, "What possible value

can speaking in tongues have if I have no idea what I am saying?'' According to the Bible, even though you do not understand what you are saying, you are praying (1 Cor. 14:14). But it is a praying with the spirit rather than the mind. It is neither an emotional nor intellectual act (although both emotion and intellect may be affected), but *an act of spiritual worship*.

It would seem that prayer in which the mind is unfruitful would have little value. What blessing can it be to pray when you have no idea what you are praying about? Actually, this is one of its greatest blessings—the fact that it is not subject to the limitations of your human intellect. The human mind, wonderful as it is from the hand of the Creator, has limited knowledge, limited linguistic ability, limited understanding, and furthermore is inhibited with all manner of prejudice. Speaking in tongues is a God-appointed manner of praying which can bypass the limitations of the intellect. One may picture the difference something like this: A prayer with the mind comes upward from the heart, and must then pass through a maze of linguistic, theological, rational, emotional, and personal check-points before it is released upward. By the time it "gets out," it may be little more than a slender trickle. An utterance in tongues comes upward from the depths, but instead of being channeled through the mind, it bypasses the mind and flows directly to God in a stream of Spirit-prompted prayer, praise, and thanksgiving.

A man came in one day and talked about this matter of praying in the Spirit, and after a while we went to the altar and prayed about it together. After a little while he began praying in tongues. He stayed at the altar by himself for some time, quietly worshipping in this new way. Afterward he told me that he had never been able to pray out loud before, not even in his private devotions. He was of Greek Orthodox background, a man without much formal education, and the most he had ever done before was to cross himself and say the Name of Jesus. "Now," he said, "I can pray as long as I want to, and it just keeps coming."

This touches on the truth which St. Paul writes about in Romans 8:26, 27: "We do not know how to pray as we ought, but the Spirit himself intercedes for us with sighs too deep for words. And he who searches the hearts of men knows what is the mind of the Spirit, because the Spirit intercedes for the saints according to the will of God." When the mind reaches that point of "not knowing how to pray as we ought," one may pray in the Spirit, trusting that the right prayer—the necessary prayer at that moment—is being offered.

Another blessing in this kind of prayer is that you are able to do it at times and in situations where normal prayer, requiring the concentration of the mind, would be impossible. A woman who worked in a garment factory told her pastor that she came out of work every night feeling inwardly polluted, because of all the foul talk which she heard around her all day long. The pastor told her to try praying silently in tongues as she did her work, which she could easily do, since praying in this way leaves the mind free to concentrate on routine tasks. She did this, and said that it was like an invisible shield had been put up around her, screening out the foul talk. She came out of work at the end of the day feeling spiritually refreshed and invigorated. Praying in tongues can be one way to help us "pray without ceasing," according to St. Paul's exhortation (1 Thess. 5:17).

"*He who speaks in a tongue edifies [builds up] himself*" (1 Cor. 14:4). This is another distinct blessing which the Bible tells us is conveyed through this gift. A woman who experienced this blessing wrote the following letter to her former pastor:

> During the past year my husband and I have felt a deepening in our spiritual lives. . . . We found ourselves searching for the truth of God and His will for us. I prayed that He would reveal His presence and give me a closer walk with Christ and fill me with the Holy Spirit. In January this year, God started answering this prayer, but not in the way I would have expected. It has worked out almost in steps which I can see now that a few months have passed by. First, He gave me a real sense of His presence but with it came this strange gift of spiritual speaking. Believe me, it was a very humbling experience. After all, I'm a college graduate and have always been grateful that I was given a good mind and a keen intellect. Instead of giving me great wisdom or understanding, which I felt I was capable of, He gave me this seemingly useless language. How could a language be useful if nobody understands it? Yet, I knew of others who had received this, and were rejoicing about it.

> Our pastor explained to me that its purpose in each individual seems to be somewhat different but in general it is most useful in one's private devotions. He encouraged me to use it in that way and to wait and see what purpose the Lord had in giving it to me.

> As the weeks went on I tried to follow this suggestion, but I became discouraged. This strange language was doing nothing for me. But gradually I became aware that my thoughts were shifting from myself and my daily activities to God and His greatness and His love for man. My everyday activities were truly being done to His service and the presence of Christ was closer to me every day. I have always tried to live my life as a service to God and to be close to Christ, but it was an effort.

It seems that God is doing these things for me. I can take no credit whatever for this change. All the glory must be to God.

Here is a person speaking spontaneously out of her own experience, without any attempt at theological reflection, yet she pinpoints accurately the meaning of this verse, "He who speaks in a tongue edifies himself."

The edification which one experiences through the exercise of speaking in tongues is on a highly individual basis. Your own program of sanctification is tailor-made by the Holy Spirit according to your individual need, and according to the place He is preparing you for in the Body of Christ. Of course this is true in a general way, whether a person speaks in tongues or not. The intellect, however, has an inveterate tendency to categorize and legalize. When the intellect steps aside, the Spirit can operate through this gift with a freer hand, building us up not where we may think we need building up, not where someone else thinks we need it, but where He, in divine wisdom, *knows* that we need building up. Exactly how or why it happens is difficult to explain, but both Scripture and experience bear out this truth: *Through this simple, yet supernatural and God-appointed way of praying, one's life in Christ is built up.*

Speaking in tongues offers a new dimension in the worship of God. "One who speaks in a tongue speaks not to men but to God . . . he utters mysteries in the Spirit" (1 Cor. 14:2). "They heard them speaking in tongues *and extolling God*" (Acts 10:46).

Even though a person who speaks in tongues doesn't understand with the mind what he is saying, he does have a clear sense of communion with God. One person has put it this way: "When I pray in English, I sometimes have to go on for quite a time before I seem to 'make contact.' In tongues I make contact almost at once, and the sense of the Presence is more real." This, of course, is a highly subjective statement. Not everyone who speaks in tongues could say the same thing, and some who do not speak in tongues could witness to a similar sense of God's presence as they pray in English, or just meditate silently. Yet it is quite generally true that the sense of communion with God, and greater freedom to express one's praise and adoration, is common with the exercise of this gift.

This new dimension in one's private worship and communion with God is surely one of the greatest blessings of speaking in tongues. It can take a variety of forms. One may "sing in the spirit," as St. Paul says, the words and melody forming together spontaneously, which can be a wonderful outpouring of the soul unto God in praise and adoration. The mood of the praying will vary from time to time, suggesting that one expresses a variety of prayers in tongues just as in his mother tongue, such as praise, adoration, thanksgiving, confession, intercession, petition, and so on.

One person became a little disturbed because he felt so burdened, almost depressed, one time as he was praying in tongues. Then it came to him that this was a prayer of confession, and as he continued praying, the burden lightened. Another person mentioned a similar experience, except that it seemed to be a burden of intercession. Perhaps these are the "sighs too deep for words" which St. Paul speaks about in Romans 8:26—things out of the reach of the understanding, things which the Spirit searches out in the heart of man and in the heart of God, and deals with through this gift.

Enhancement of one's private worship is a great blessing of speaking in tongues. The other blessings are summed up in it: *As you worship God in tongues, your mind is at rest and your spirit prays, unhindered by the limitations of the human understanding, and through this act of worship the Holy Spirit builds up your life in Christ.*

Questions and Problems

No gift of the Holy Spirit is so freighted with doubts, misgivings, questions, and misunderstandings as speaking in tongues. We want to consider these questions honestly and objectively, under the heading of three words which loom large wherever speaking in tongues comes up for discussion: Emotionalism, Overemphasis, Divisiveness.

Emotionalism

"Doesn't speaking in tongues open the door to a lot of uncontrolled emotionalism? In churches with a dignified and restrained worship tradition—such as Lutheran, Episcopalian, Presbyterian, Catholic—this question can give rise to real disturbance, both for the individual Christian and for the congregation.

One man told how his mother had belonged to a church where speaking in tongues was practiced. As a child he was taken to meetings in the church. He saw people shaking, screaming, actually rolling on the floor—often in connection with speaking in tongues. Memories like this are hard to erase. This man, as he grew up, turned adamantly against this whole manner of religious expression, and vowed to have nothing more to do with it.

In spite of this considerable and well-grounded prejudice, however, he later came to the conviction that God wanted him to have the gift of speaking in tongues. He prayed and received it. But when he spoke in tongues, it was calm and unemotional—

just a quiet speaking, with an undertone of joy. His witness as to what this has meant in his life and ministry has the same note of quiet restraint, and yet it has become precious and real in his own life.

The manner in which a person expresses the gift of tongues is not determined primarily by the gift itself. It is largely determined by the individual and by the religious setting. If a man worships in a religious setting where the emotions are expressed in a loud and exuberant fashion, and if he himself is similarly inclined, then he will likely express speaking in tongues in this way. (He would also put the same feeling into singing "The Old Rugged Cross.") But if he has grown up in a religious setting where the quieter emotions of awe and reverence have been cultivated, he is likely to speak in tongues in a more reserved way.

In a prayer group of Lutherans and Episcopalians, for example, the speaking in tongues may be no more pronounced in its emotional aspect than prayers in English. The reason speaking in tongues is tied to emotionalism in many people's minds is because the practice of it in classical Pentecostalism has been primarily among groups which follow a rather free and emotional form of worship.

Perhaps a further reason for this misconception is that in the Bible speaking in tongues is primarily associated with the church at Corinth. In this congregation, lack of inhibition seemed to be the order of the day. Nor was it limited to the exercise of speaking in tongues. In the eleventh chapter, we read that they were getting drunk at Holy Communion. Here, again, it was not the gift which led to emotionalism, but rather, the gift was being used in a setting where people were already disposed toward this kind of expression.

A third reason for this misconception lies in the

frequent use of the term "ecstatic utterance" as a synonym for speaking in tongues. There is no warrant in Scripture for the use of this term to describe speaking in tongues. It is always referred to simply as a 'speaking.' The Greek word *ekstasis*, the root of our English "ecstasy," is never used to describe a speaker in tongues. On two occasions in Acts this word is used to describe those who *hear* someone speak in tongues, and is usually translated "amazed." The idea that a speaker in tongues goes into a kind of religious ecstasy, where he loses emotional and personal control, is contrary both to Scripture and actual experience. The person who exercises this gift is perfectly able to remain in full control of himself and his emotions. If he weren't, St. Paul would not be able to give such direct and down-to-earth instruction as he does in 1 Corinthians 14:28, "If there is no one to interpret, let the speaker in tongues keep silence in church and speak to himself and to God."

Overemphasis

"Isn't speaking in tongues overemphasized whenever it comes on the scene?"

This is often the case. It can be and has been overemphasized. The reason for this overemphasis seems to be twofold.

The first reason is readily understandable. Speaking in tongues can be a deeply moving personal experience, opening up new spiritual horizons. Any person who has this kind of experience is eager to share it with others. For a time he may overdo it. We see this same kind of thing in people who are newly converted.

A man was converted while he was in the Navy, and he came home all fired up to convert his family and friends. The wife said, a little wryly, "We lost most of our friends that first year."

In the first flush of experience, speaking in tongues may come to have a disproportionate emphasis in a congregation, or in the personal life and witness of an individual. The answer to this kind of thing is wise and understanding pastoral guidance. First of all, a pastor or friend should honestly *rejoice* in the person's experience (1 Cor. 12:26). At the same time, it must be pointed out that this is only one aspect of the Faith. It should not become the focal point of one's life or witness.

Indeed, it is often wise to keep one's experience of speaking in tongues as a "holy secret" for a time, until it has a chance to root down in one's life. Talking about spiritual experiences too freely can be detrimental to one's continued growth. Furthermore, one needs to live with this experience, as with any experience, for some time before he is able to give a balanced impression of it to someone else.

To share it with a wise and understanding friend, however, is not only right but probably necessary. Such a friend, ideally the person's own pastor, or spiritual counselor can share the joy, and then also offer the kind of counsel which will help knit this experience into the total fabric of one's Christian life.

When people receive this kind of pastoral care, they do not give speaking in tongues undue emphasis in their testimony or converstaion. They are more likely to talk about the Lord, or about some new discovery in the Bible, than about speaking in tongues.

A second reason for overemphasis is more difficult to deal with. Sometimes real antagonism rises up toward speaking in tongues as such, or towards those who advocate it. This no doubt springs from a variety of causes, but when it is present it leads to a kind of negative overemphasis of the gift. The gift is constantly pushed into the spotlight by argument and debate *against* it. This will more than likely evoke a defensive reaction on the part of those who value the gift.

Suppose a man came to work in a factory where all of the employees had only four fingers on each hand—the little finger was missing. The other employees soon notice that he has a little finger. At first it evokes some curiosity, but before long also some antagonism.

"You don't need to think you're any better than we are just because you have a little finger."

"Well, I like it—"

"We've gotten along without little fingers in this factory for a long time!"

The man shrugs and lets the matter drop. But every time he's on a lunch or coffee break, someone begins to question or challenge him about his little finger.

"We can work the machines with our four fingers just as well as you can. What good is that little finger anyway?"

"Well, it's the way God made me, and I find it helpful."

"It's causing all sorts of argument and trouble in the plant. Why don't you cut it off and be like the rest of us?"

"No, I don't want to. It's part of my body. I like my little finger."

This little finger is tremendously overemphasized as to its real importance *because it is constantly being challenged.* The overemphasis comes not because of the *use* of the little finger, but because of its mere *presence.*

This kind of overemphasis often occurs in connection with speaking in tongues. People who may never have heard a person speak in tongues stir up argument and discussion concerning it. Even when those who speak in tongues would be happy to let the matter rest, it is continually brought up to be challenged and questioned. When someone has received a blessing from God and then has that blessing challenged as though it were something foolish or worthless, he will naturally speak out to defend that blessing.

The perfect answer to this situation is given in 1 Corinthians 12:26: "If one member is honored, all rejoice together." If other members of the congregation can *honestly rejoice* with those who receive this gift, a lot of overemphasis will be put quietly to rest. If those who speak in tongues find themselves in a welcome and understanding environment, their own tendency toward overemphasis can be dealt with more effectively.

Divisiveness

"Why does speaking in tongues so often result in divisiveness?" Denominatons, congregations, even families, get split up over it. What's behind it?

Lutheran pastor K. G. Egertson made this observation: "The cause of divisiveness is that those either 'for' or 'against' become militant." This is an incisive insight into the real cause for divisiveness: It is not speaking in tongues that is divisive. (We could hardly attribute divisiveness to a gift from the Holy Spirit! He would not inject a divisive element into the church which He is sanctifying!) The cause of divisiveness is always to be found in the ignorance and sinfulness of man, coupled with the agitation of Satan.

If an objective observer were to enter a situation where divisiveness had occurred over speaking in tongues, he would likely find two dynamics at work, in varying proportions, depending upon the particular situation:

(1) Lack of wisdom, decency, and order in the use of the gift, or in conversation and witnessing concerning it.

(2) A rejection, suppression, or mere tolerance of the gift in the congregation.

Scripture warns against both of these extremes. Turning to the left, St. Paul says, "Let all things be done decently and in order" (1 Cor. 14:40). Turning to the right he says, "Quench not the Spirit; despise not prophesying; forbid not speaking in tongues" (1 Thess. 5:19, 20; 1 Cor. 14:39).

A Study Commission of the American Lutheran Church, appointed to look into the question of speaking in tongues, called attention to these two factors:

> It is possible to have unity with diversity if Christ is Lord and His love reigns over all. A statement such as "speaking in tongues is not Lutheran" does not make for a better spirit in the congregation, nor does the "If-you-don't-like-it-lump-it" attitude.[90]

If people involved in a situation of divisiveness—especially church officials, pastors, and lay leaders of a congregation—see clearly these two dynamics, they will have gone a long way toward bringing about a spirit of love and harmony. They will speak a word of admonition to those who *have* experienced the gift and a word to those who have *not*. When the responsibilities of each are clearly drawn out, and accepted, the conditions for peace and harmony are present.

Lutheran theologian George Aus wrote this kind of advice to our congregation when we were wrestling with this question:

To those who *have* experienced the gift: 1) Be sure that the purpose for which you use it is positive, i.e., for edification—whether private or corporate. 2) Let the Spirit sift your motives in the public use of the gift. 3) One of the risks in this gift is that it can become divisive. Be in prayer that if it becomes divisive it be not due to you—or your use of the gift, e.g., when it is used to exalt self in the display of spiritual excellence. 4) Beware of spiritual pride.

To those who have *not* experienced the gift: 1) If the exercise of the gift by others edifies you— thank God. 2) Do not be disturbed by the fact that it has not been given to you. This fact does not mean that something is wrong with you or that you are an inferior or carnal Christian. 3) Your function in the edification of the congregation may call for other gifts. What kind of a body would it be if everyone were a foot?

We have seen this kind of advice work out within a single family. The wife had experienced the gift, the husband had not. She was happy in her experience, and grew as a result of it, but she did not overplay it. He, on the other hand, genuinely rejoiced with her, even though he himself had not received the gift. He also grew spiritually. Harmony on this basis is no theory, but a definite possibility and reality.

If those who speak in tongues are modest and orderly, and if those who do not speak in tongues accept the presence of the gift in the congregation, and rejoice with those who have received it, the congregation will be knit together in peace and harmony.

Healing

To the Church at Corinth St. Paul wrote, "If I preach the gospel, that gives me no ground for boasting. For *necessity* is laid upon me. Woe to me if

I do not preach the gospel . . . [for] *I am entrusted with a commission"* (1 Cor. 9:16).

In the same letter Paul describes what he means by "the preaching of the gospel": "My speech and my message were not in plausible words of wisdom, *but in demonstration of the Spirit and of power,* that your faith might not rest in the wisdom of man *but in the power of God"* (1 Cor. 2:4).

In the New Testament we catch a glimpse here and there of Paul's apostleship. At Lystra he was preaching to a group of people and one of the men listening to him could not use his feet. He was a cripple from birth. Paul looked at him intently and said, "Stand up on your feet" (Acts 14:10). And the man sprang up and walked. He sprang up and walked because the preaching of Paul was more than a statement of certain theological truths: It was a vehicle of power.

In Ephesus the Lord did extraordinary miracles by the hand of Paul. They would even take handkerchiefs or aprons which he had touched and carry them to the sick, and diseases left them and evil spirits came out of them (Acts 19:11-12). The diseases left them and evil spirits came out of them because Paul did more than teach them a philosophy of life: He put them in touch with the healing power of God.

On the island of Malta Paul visited the father of a leading citizen, who lay sick with fever and dysentery. He put his hand on him and healed him. And when this had taken place, the rest of the people on the island who had diseases also came and were cured (Acts 28:8-9). They were cured because the gospel Paul preached was not a gospel of mere words: It was a gospel of power.

Paul had no fear of speaking the command of faith to a cripple, sending the healing power of God streaming into his withered legs; he had no fear of ministering healing to the sick and possessed in Ephesus and on the island of Malta. Paul had no fear of preaching and ministering in the manifest power of God. But he did have a holy fear of preaching the gospel merely in the power of human wisdom and eloquence—"not with eloquent wisdom, lest the cross of Christ be emptied of its power" (1 Cor. 1:17).

Much present-day preaching of the gospel is exactly reversed. We hold no fear of preaching the gospel with a brilliant display of human wisdom and eloquence: Flawless progression of logic and rhetoric, replete with historical and literary allusions, psychologically persuasive, intellectually respectable, philosophically palatable, appealing to one's sense of morality and responsibility, emotionally uplifting. This kind of preaching can go on week after week, month after month, year after year—faultless in form and even thoroughly orthodox in doctrine—yet with no manifestation of God's power whatever. Do we *fear* this kind of preaching, as Paul did? We don't. We admire it! Laymen stand in awe, and preachers in envy. But let the *power* of God so much as be mentioned—prayers for healing, anointing with oil, exorcism, the demonstration of the Spirit—just mention this, and people draw back in fear and doubt.

As you talk with people throughout the church, you tend to find either an outright fear and opposition to a ministry of healing, or at best an attitude of reserved tolerance: "It's all right for those who have a special interest along this line, providing you don't talk about it too much or try to promote it in any way, and it doesn't interfere with all of the regular church programs." In other words, it's an extra, a frill; it's an optional feature tacked onto the church's regular business of preaching the gospel.

Would St. Paul agree with that evaluation? Would

he separate the preaching of the gospel from the ministry of healing? Are they not two aspects of the same thing? preaching is the gospel in *word,* healing is the gospel in *action,* They are both necessary. If you have healing without preaching, it can degenerate into spiritism and psychic experimentation. And if you have preaching without healing, that can degenerate into lifeless creeds and dogmas, a religion of dead ritual and tradition.

The charismatic renewal is one of the voices being raised today, urging the church to practice a ministry of healing as a normal aspect of proclaiming the gospel.

Healing and the Will of God

In considering a ministry of healing in the church, we must face up to a very elemental question: *Is healing according to the will of God?*

Several factors lead us to a positive answer to that question. First, Jesus himself carried on an active ministry of healing. It is not true, as some contend, that Jesus healed only as a "sign" that He was the Son of God. He healed to fulfill what the prophets had described His ministry to be (Matt. 8:17). He healed not to prove that He was the Son of God, but because He was the Son of God. He healed just because He was Jesus, the One desiring to defeat those things which sin had brought into the community of people rightly belonging to Him. "He had compassion on him and healed him" (Mark 1:40 ff.).

The healing ministry of the church proceeds from the indwelling Christ, who makes the Body sharer in His compassion: "When one member of the body suffers, all suffer together" (1 Cor. 12:25). There is no word in Scripture which suggests that healing would outdo its usefulness in the church, or in glorifying God. Jesus healed. He has never said, "I do not desire to heal any longer." It is men who have presumed by human reason toward this conclusion. Yet where God has been honored by those who trust His word, He in turn has honored that faith, and worked healings.

The Presbyterian Church in America, in a report adopted by its General Convention, said: "Jesus healed out of mercy in the knowledge that it is God's will to deliver men from all kinds of evil, including physical and mental illness. The evidence of this is the attention he gave to the sick and to the handicapped and what he said about these works. If he had believed that disease and death were parts of God's ultimate purpose, he would surely not have carried out a ministry of healing. Far from acquiescing to suffering or deprivation, he prayed and worked for its removal. He regarded the healings which took place as so many signs of God's power breaking in upon the kingdom of evil . . . he considered the conquest of sickness and infirmity to be God's will." [91]

Jesus specifically ascribed sickness to the activity of Satan in Luke 13:16, as He healed the woman with a crooked spine. His work in casting out demons He described as "plundering Satan's kingdom" (Luke 11:14). In a case where the cause of sickness was not ascribed to sin or Satan, Jesus nevertheless healed the man (John 9:7).

Consider the question from a purely practical point-of-view: What do you do when you or a member of your family falls seriously ill? Without hesitation, without doubt or qualm, do you not at once call a doctor? And what will the doctor do when he comes? Will he not work toward this one objective: *to restore the sick person to health?* If you truly doubt that God wills your healing, dare you call the doctor—for you know that he will work with every means at his command *for healing?* If God does not will your healing, then you will be actively working against His will in calling the doctor.

In this practical situation neither we nor the doctor seriously question that God's will is to overcome disease and bring healing. Yet many Christians use this as a convenient excuse to avoid facing up to the responsibility and challenge of a ministry of healing in the church.

A further point: An Episcopalian minister, Edgar L. Sanford, helped bring this issue into focus by concentrating our attention not on the will of God, as such, but upon man's responsibility in the face of illness—namely, *to seek health,* by all means at his disposal, spiritual as well as medical. In *God's Healing Power,* he said, "Some people say of an illness that it is the will of God . . . it is inevitable that our world will bring us face to face with illness, perils, discouragements. Often these things are our own fault or the result of someone else's bad choosing. Sometimes they are due to circumstances beyond anyone's control. But God does not will them for us because He thinks that they will be good for us, or for any other reason. . . . God will assist you to live victoriously if you seek His help. In this, He is like a good earthly father who will not hurt his child's integrity by overprotecting him and removing all his ills for him, but who is always ready to guide and help him as circumstances require. To countless people, Jesus is not only the expression of God's will but also the true pattern for man's behavior. And a considerable part of His ministry was devoted to overcoming illness. This then would seem to be the will of God: *not that men be sick but that they SEEK TO BE WELL AND HELP OTHERS TO BE WELL.* And this is where the soul's growth takes place, not in being ill but in doing what you can to overcome illness. . . . Spiritual healing, then, is an adventure of the soul to see what can be done to overcome an illness; and God is as interested in the project as the sick person is." [92]

What Did Jesus Intend for the Church?

Is there any real doubt that the Lord intended His church to be a healing church?

The gospel records no single case where the Lord Jesus himself either refused or failed to heal a sick person who came to Him. When He sent the twelve disciples out on their first mission, He gave them the specific command to heal the sick (Luke 9:2). At the end of His earthly life Jesus told His disciples that when they went out into the world, they would do the works He had done—and even greater works, because He would be sending them the Holy Spirit (John 14:12). The Great Commission includes the command, "Teach them to observe all that I have commanded you" (Matt. 28:20). Healing was clearly one of the things Jesus had commanded them, and therefore as much a part of the Commission as preaching and teaching.

The rest of the New Testament leaves us no doubt that the apostles took Jesus at His word, in a simple and realistic way. They *did* the works of Jesus—including the works of healing. In the Epistle of St. James we see how healing had become accepted and practiced as a part of the ministry of any normal Christian congregation. A congregation without a healing ministry would have been as out of place in New Testament times as Lutherans without confirmation.

Healing was never meant to be an option in the Christian Church—something that's all right for those who like to go off on special tangents. The ministry of healing is part of the gospel, and therefore it is an obligation. "Woe to me if I do not preach the gospel—the gospel in all its truth and all its power— woe to me if I do not preach *this* gospel . . . for I have been entrusted with a commission" (1 Cor. 9:16, 17).

An officer commissioned into the armed services of his country doesn't pick and choose among the orders sent down to him, obeying those he agrees with and neglecting those he disagrees with or does not fully understand. He obeys every order that comes down. Whether he likes it, understands the reasons behind it, or agrees with it makes no real difference: *His commission is a commission unto obedience.*

People raise many questions and objections concerning the ministry of healing. "Oh, it can lead to fanaticism! People might lose their faith if you pray for someone and then he dies! We have modern medicine now and don't need healing by prayer! Faith healers are all quacks anyway!" There *are* dangers in the ministry of healing. There have been abuses. But the *neglect* of the ministry of healing has a danger that outweighs them all: *the danger of disobeying the Lord.*

"Is any among you sick? Pray for them, that they may be healed" (James 5:14). This is the word of God. *The issue before the church is one of simple obedience to her Lord.*

The Basis for Obedience: The Word of God

Ever since the Garden of Eden, man has rebelled against giving simple obedience to the Lord. Ever since the Garden of Eden, man has sought to order his life by knowledge and reason and human understanding, rather than by simple obedience to the Word of God.

What happened back there? God planted the Garden of Eden, and in the midst of the garden He set a certain tree. The Lord told Adam and Eve that they could eat of the fruit of every tree in the garden except of that certain tree in the midst of the garden— the tree of the knowledge of good and evil.

God did not declare knowledge, as such, to be off limits for man. Between the creation of man and his fall into sin, Adam no doubt acquired a good deal of knowledge about the world in which God had placed him. He began to discover many of the laws and principles which govern our natural world, and to apply this knowledge in a useful way. God laid the whole natural realm out before man, and in this realm analysis and reason and understanding was perfectly proper. Scientific investigation was God's appointed way for man to discover the truth about the natural world in which he lived—to observe, investigate, analyze, and explore the whole physical universe.

What then was forbidden to man by the word of the Lord? Forbidden to him was the fruit of the tree of the knowledge *of good and evil.*

The knowledge of good and evil does not belong to the natural realm, where man has perfect freedom to investigate and seek knowledge; it belongs to the moral and spiritual realm. And *this* realm God did *not* lay out for man to analyze and investigate. In fact, He warned man that knowledge from this realm boded great danger. "In the day that you eat of [the tree of the knowledge of good and evil] you shall die" (Gen. 2:17).

God put the knowledge of good and evil off limits for man, because He knew that He had not created man to operate and function in the spiritual realm the same way he did in the natural realm. In the natural realm man's inquisitiveness and investigation and knowledge would lead him to truth about that natural realm. But in the spiritual realm that same inquisitiveness and investigation and knowledge would lead to death. God ordained a different way for man to learn the truth about the spiritual realm; truth in the spiritual realm was to come not by investigation and knowledge, but by *revelation*.

What is truth in the natural realm? Truth is what you seek out and learn and prove by knowledge and reason. And what is truth in the spiritual realm? *Truth is what God has spoken.* Both are equally true. And the truth in both cases is equally of God, for He is the creator and sustainer of both realms. But the truth from these two realms comes to man in two different ways: From the natural realm by way of reason, from the spiritual realm by way of revelation.

These two ways of truth cannot be mixed. If you want to learn the truth about the natural realm, you go after it by the methods of inquiry and investigation. If you get into your auto some morning and it won't start, you don't sit there and wait for a voice from heaven to reveal to you what's wrong, nor do you begin leafing quickly through the book of Leviticus to see if you can get some guidance on what you ought to do. You get out there under the hood and begin checking the battery and spark plugs and distributor; if need be, you call a mechanic who knows more about it than you do. It would be silly to wait around for revelation when God has put the truth right under your nose to be discovered.

This silly illustration points up how foolish it is to try to lay hold on the natural realm by the method of revelation—which belongs to the spiritual realm. But it is equally foolish to reverse the process and try and lay hold on the spiritual realm by human wisdom and knowledge—the method which belongs to the natural realm. St. Paul says that it pleased God that the world by its wisdom should not know God (1 Cor. 1:21). Ever since the Garden of Eden human reason has supposed that it could encompass anything—even the secret things of God. But the Bible says, "The secret things belong to the Lord our God; but the things that are revealed belong to us and to our children for ever" (Deut. 29:29). We can know just that amount of truth from the spiritual realm which God chooses to reveal to us—and with that revelation we are to be content. In the Garden of Eden God intended that Adam and Eve should be content with the simple revelation that the tree in the midst of the garden was not to be touched. It was when the Tempter lured them into using their human reason to begin questioning and doubting the revelation that they got into trouble. The question led to doubt, doubt led to disobedience, and disobedience led to death. Trying to bring the spiritual realm down to the level of human understanding is worse than foolish: It is an invitation to tragedy, defeat, and death.

Let an example from another epoch of our faith point this up. Imagine the situation among the people of Israel in Egypt when Moses was about to lead them out of slavery, and had given them the Lord's instructions regarding the Passover (Ex. 12:1-27). Imagine someone speaking up there, trying to bring a little reason and common sense to bear on this whole business—

"Now, Moses, *really*—killing a lamb and smearing its blood on our doorposts and lintels—what possible good is *that* going to do? That doesn't make sense. If we're going to get out of this place, we've got to go and make a deal with Pharaoh. . ."

We know what the result would have been of following such a counsel of reason and common sense. It would have been death.

Human wisdom boasts great things, but whenever it tries to master the spiritual realm it flounders helplessly. Solomon recognized this back in Old Testament times: "Trust in the Lord with all your heart, and do not rely on your own insight" (Prov. 3:5). In the spiritual realm your own insight, independent of God's revelation, is not competent to guide you. Jeremiah saw it too: "I know, O Lord, that the way of man is not in himself, that it is not in man who walks to direct his [own] steps." (Jer. 10:23) Human understanding can't make head nor tail out of spiritual truth. The truth and wisdom of the spiritual realm actually seems to be utter foolishness to our worldly wisdom. Martin Luther once said, "The world owes the gospel a grudge because the gospel condemns the wisdom of the world." The gospel comes to you with a truth which human wisdom simply cannot grasp. In the presence of the revelation of God, human wisdom can only bow down with the Psalmist, and say, "Such knowledge is too wonderful for me; it is high, I cannot attain it" (Ps. 139:6).

Consider the very heart of our Christian faith: Does it make any sense to human reason that the shedding of blood should have anything to do with forgiving sin and relieving guilt? And doesn't it make even less sense when you are told that the blood was shed over 1900 years ago, in a little out-of-the-way corner of the great Roman Empire? What possible connection can there be between that event and this guilt that's bothering me? Human reason counsels us to dismiss this as a superstitious relic from antiquity. But a Christian knows from experience that he doesn't have to understand that mystery.

He can experience the cleansing power of that blood though he can't begin to explain it.

It is no different with spiritual healing. Though human reason cannot encompass its working, a simple believer can obediently bring the sick to the Lord —and they will experience God's healing power.

What is the conclusion of all this? God does not reveal the truth of the spiritual realm in order to satisfy our curiosity and give us some abstract knowledge about that realm (we get a bit of that quite incidentally). God's purpose in revealing the truth of the spiritual realm is that we might *obey* Him, and thereby experience the *power* of that realm. "The secret things belong to God, but the things that are revealed belong to us, and to our children for ever, that we may *do* all the words of this law..." (Deut. 29:29).

The "word of the cross" which Paul speaks about in 1 Corinthians is not God's explanation about certain relationships and truths in the spiritual realm (that comes as a by-product). But the "word of the cross... is the *power of God*" (1 Cor. 1:18). The tragedy in much of present-day Christianity is that we have been content to let the revelation give us a smattering of knowledge of the spiritual realm— doctrines and definitions, which are purely incidental —while God's purpose is to give us *power*.

Why is the power of the early church so lacking in our churches today? Why is the church today unable to say with St. Paul, "My message... is in demonstration of the Spirit and power"? (1 Cor. 2:3). Why is the ministry of healing still considered by many to be an activity for fanatical cults and sects outside the church? Does not the answer lie in this very thing we have considered? We have sought to lay hold on the spiritual realm with the inadequate tools of human knowledge and reason.

We have dragged the revelation of God down to the level of human possibility, to the level of our meager experience, to the level of our human questions, doubts, and speculations.

There is a basic law for getting along in the spiritual realm, and that law is this: *Trust and obey the Word of God.* Don't water it down and demean it to the level of our human doubts and possibilities. Rather, let the Word of God lift the situation to the level of *God's* possibilities. If there was one thing Job learned through all his troubles, it was this: Man does not call God into question and judgment before the bar of human reason. "I lay my hand upon my mouth. I have spoken once . . . I will proceed no further. I have uttered what I did not understand: things too wonderful for me, which I did not know" (Job 40:4, 42:3). The failure of the church to demonstrate the Spirit and manifest the power of God stems from her unwillingness to trust and obey the Word of God.

Spiritual healing is a thing "too wonderful, which we do not know." It is a thing which leads us into many difficult questions, into many hours of deep and difficult and soul-searching prayer. But it leads us, also, into a living relationship with Him who is "the same yesterday and today and forever" (Heb. 13:8). Most important, it leads us into faithful obedience to the Word of God, and precisely therein lies its greatest blessing.

Prophecy, Vision, Revelation

The charismatic renewal has recalled the church to more spontaneous modes of revelation, a wholesome complement to the emphasis on purely rational processes and conclusions. This is not to downgrade serious intellectual work, but rather to recognize that God may speak to the church in a variety of ways.

Prophecy, vision, and spontaneous revelation are elements of the Christian heritage which the charismatic renewal has sought to recover for the church.

These gifts can function in a natural and practical way in the context of prayer and personal ministry. Either privately or during special prayer services people can come to members of the congregation who are able to pray for them not only according to request, but also by spontaneous revelation.

This kind of ministry is unfamiliar to many Lutherans, but it holds great potential for blessing. By spontaneous revelation God is able to confirm and reinforce truth which has particular application to a person's life. A young woman once attended a personal ministry service in a Lutheran church. She appeared outwardly composed. However, the elder who prayed for her, though he did not know her personally, discerned a strong spirit of anger, and sensed that she faced a major decision. As this spontaneous revelation impressed itself upon him, a word of warning unfolded in his mind.

"A decision which proceeds out of anger can have great force," he said, "but its direction is likely to be faulty."

The woman recognized this as a word of wisdom, and it helped her to reevaluate a major decision she was contemplating.

This kind of ministry, of course, must be exercised with mature Christian judgment, and must be measured by the norm of Scripture. Where a congregation provides this kind of a setting, a ministry of prayer and revelation can develop in a good way and be a blessing to many.

The fact that these gifts are "inspired by the Holy Spirit" (1 Cor. 12:11) does not mean that there should not be teaching which will help develop and perfect the use of the gifts. In 1 Corinthians 12-14, the apostle gives a whole series of practical instructions for the right use of spiritual gifts. As congregations become open to the manifestation of spiritual gifts, there must be a corresponding teaching to insure that they will develop and be used in a good way.

One Lutheran congregation printed the following instructions for members who were called to this kind of a ministry—[93]

Principles of Spiritual Perception

How does God communicate with us? How does spontaneous revelation actually come? Here are some pointers from Scripture and experience:

1. *Pictures.* God often spoke to prophets through pictures or visions. He may plant a picture in your mind that has special meaning for you. If you "walk around it," as it were, the central meaning of that picture or scene will come to you. Once a strong picture of Ruth, in the Old Testament, came to mind while praying for a young woman. The person praying said something like this: "I get the feeling that you are somehow a Ruth-like person . . ." The woman broke down crying. She had been praying about her relationship with her mother-in-law, and had asked for more love, such as Ruth had for Naomi. The person ministering had never met her before. This is the kind of direct and pointed ministry which can open up when we step out in faith.

Many people get pictures like this without knowing they are from God. Jeremiah saw two baskets of figs, Amos saw a basket of summer fruit, Peter saw a sheet, Daniel saw a giant statue; most of the book of Revelation came in picture form. Our deep mind responds to this kind of symbolic language. If we are willing to concentrate on getting quiet and letting God speak, He will do so. Be careful not to tear into the picture with the hacksaw of reason. Let the interpretation come naturally.

If you are praying with someone when a picture comes, it is normally good to wait until the significance becomes clear to you. Sometimes this will be more-or-less obvious, such as a yo-yo symbolizing an up-and-down experience, or a fire suggesting purifying. Sometimes the symbol will be more personal, or the meaning less clear. It may be that someone else will need to contribute to the interpretation, either another one ministering, or the person being prayed for. In some cases no particular or significant meaning unfolds, in which case it is perfectly all right to pray a more general blessing.

2. *Scripture.* God speaks through specific Bible verses which come to mind. He may impress a part of a verse or even a reference upon your mind.

3. *A word.* A common phrase in the writings of the prophets is: "The word of the Lord came to..." One prophet said: "He laid a word in my mouth." Another was constrained to speak because the words burned within him.

God may bring to your mind a specific word or piece of advice that did not come as the result of a detailed thought process. It was more spontaneous and 'given,' as if dropped into your mind. Oftentimes in praying for another, as you begin to share the word given you, more of the message becomes clear.

The thoughts that come in this way from the Lord are usually unpremeditated and spontaneous in character, and come more in a flash without a logical sequence, whereas when we are consciously thinking, or even daydreaming, we usually connect one thought with another.

Remember, we "prophesy in part." Don't be afraid to launch out for fear you may say something that does not hit right on target. Through experience we learn. In the Body of Christ, others can help as they "weigh what is said" (1 Cor. 14:28).

Sometimes it is necessary to do a little 'fishing,' to ask the person to whom you are ministering whether such-and-such an area in his life is causing any problems, whether he is facing some kind of an important decision, etc. Your revelation may be a little general, and this will help you to understand more specifically what the Lord may be giving you at the time.

Preparation for Ministry

1. Prepare your heart. Do some spiritual calisthenics before the ministry, when possible; yet remain flexible on the field. God may use something He gives you that day or something that has been coming to you as a theme through the previous week, yet always seek to be sensitive to the word of the Lord for now.

2. Empty yourself out through confession. God's word flows through empty vessels. Then, having received forgiveness, minister in the state and awareness of forgiveness.

3. Expect God to use you. Believe that you have the mind of Christ and that God will speak clearly to you and through you. Fear of not getting a word, or of giving a wrong word, paralyzes faith and makes your spirit restless. Jesus said, "My sheep hear my voice." Realize that God deeply loves the people coming for ministry and He will get through to them. Remember that a prophetic gift functions according to the faith of the prophet.

4. Earnestly desire the spiritual gifts, and especially that you may prophesy. Pray that God will give you a spirit of revelation.

5. *Be willing to step out.* Practice prophesying in groups and settings where it is appropriate. We develop the spiritual gifts by using them, not by waiting for the heavens to be opened before we step out.

6. Be willing to fail. Say to yourself, "I do not care if I stumble. I am willing to be corrected. I love these people and want them to get a word from God."

7. Lay aside your personal needs and problems. Do not minister out of the need of your present circumstances. Let God dictate your mood and ministry, not your personal situation.

During Ministry . . .

1. Do not assume that you know a person's need because you know his problem. Erase it from your mind and stay

in neutral. God will usually give something new if you do not prejudge a word.

2. Do not offend with bad breath. Take the necessary precautions.

3. When anointing with oil for healing, either because they request it or because you know they are sick and feel the situation calls for it, quote James 5:14-16. Then ask the sick person if he is aware of any sin that might block healing, and if so, to confess it. Anoint him by putting a small amount of oil on your right index finger and applying it to his forehead, making the sign of the cross as you say, "I anoint you with oil in the name of the Father, and of the Son, and of the Holy Spirit." Then pray specifically for healing.

4. Be careful of passivity when waiting for a word. Do not simply coast along. Be spiritually alert. Seek the word of the Lord for this person.

5. Some people have a special gift to read a person's spirit. You may wish to pray, "Lord, what is the condition of their spirit and how can I help you meet their need?"

6. Do not expect that God will necessarily speak to you the way He does to others. He may use a word, a picture, an impression, a feeling, a Scripture, or He may be silent.

7. *Do not counsel with people;* counseling is another kind of ministry. Your ministry here should generally be short and to the point. Avoid the shotgun approach of unloading both barrels. Seek rather to pinpoint the word of the Lord for this person so that he is clear on the "take-away" word. The word can get lost if you speak too long.

8. Be sensitive to people's needs. It is difficult for many to kneel for more than a short time.

9. Avoid long pauses. If nothing comes you may wish to ask the individual if he has any needs. Or you may pray a general prayer of encouragement, have a brief time of praise, or simply "jump in" and expect God to pinpoint a word as you begin to speak.

10. Some find that speaking quietly in tongues helps to release the word of prophecy. It prepares the mind to operate in this spiritual dimension.

11. Refine the word before giving it. Interpret the pic-

ture rather than giving it and asking them to do the interpreting. Present a picture you do not understand only if an interpretation does not come to you, but you feel that either another minister or the recipient may understand the word. A general symbolic picture can probably be immediately explained, but a picture that would need explaining, such as one out of your past experience, needs interpretation.

12. When you feel that you need to give a hard word, pray for divine tact. Make sure that you are not personally involved; the word needs to have objective authority.

13. Avoid the extremes of "Thus saith the Lord..." on the one hand and the other extreme of not having any authority when you speak. Let the authority of the word be in the word given, not in our personal prefixes or suffixes to the word.

14. Summarize the word in a sentence or two when you have finished ministering to the person. This will help him focus upon its meaning and application afterwards.

Spiritual Gifts and the Means of Grace

For the most part, the charismatic renewal has avoided the pitfalls of the enthusiasts, the "super spirituals," who vexed Luther. They looked for the Spirit in their own dreams of a spiritual world above, missing the God who has chosen to reveal himself in the humility of external signs.[94] Indeed, as Lutheran theologian Karlfried Froehlich has pointed out, the charismatic emphasis can actually serve to counteract unbridled religious enthusiasm—

> In His freedom God made himself flesh in the humbleness of down-to-earth, external phenomena— bread, wine, water, word. The Spirit, a person of the Trinity, cannot be thought to be found on another level. This opens the road to a legitimate location of charismatic manifestations within the framework of the Lutheran Confessions.

Could the charismatic phenomena of our day be seen as manifestations of the Spirit in a new, concrete human form? Could the yearning of Christians for the experience of charismatic phenomena be understood as part of that incarnational emphasis, the longing for something concrete, real, down-to-earth to express what has been there in a lofty way already?

Could it be that Martin Luther himself would side with the charismatic movement in the church today for precisely the same reasons that forced him to reject what he saw as the flight from this earth in the Enthusiasts? [95]

The enthusiasts were ready to set Scripture aside in favor of their own revelations. This finds no parallel in the charismatic renewal, where the Bible functions as the fountain, rule, and norm for faith and life. If anything, charismatics may be criticized for a too-literalistic reading of the Bible. But there is no voice in the renewal proposing that Scripture be set to the side in favor of direct (or further) revelations of the Spirit. Charismatics would agree wholeheartedly with Luther that the Spirit has tied himself to the external Word.

Another way of putting it would be: The redemptive activity of the Spirit is shaped according to the Word. A scene in the movie *Patton* portrays the American tank general foiling a major attack of Rommel's Afrika Korps. At the end of the battle Patton exults, "Rommel, I read your book!" He knew that the Germans' basic strategy would be shaped according to Rommel's book on tank warfare. This illustration is inappropriate in that the Holy Spirit is not our opponent but our friend. But setting that literalism aside, it suggests the kind of relationship which exists between the Holy Spirit and the Word: The Word describes the basic way in which we may expect the Holy Spirit to behave; the kind of objectives He has, the way He goes about achieving those objectives. He will not act contrary to nor outside of that which He has caused to be revealed and proclaimed in the external Word.

The external Word is more than the Bible, though it flows forth from the Bible and conforms to it. It is the word of the gospel that is preached, prayed, spoken, taught, witnessed to, confirmed by signs following, demonstrated in the sacraments—the word flowing from the fountain of Scripture, which the Holy Spirit makes alive.

The Word does not only describe the Holy Spirit's redemptive activity, but is instrumental in carrying it out. It tells us what to expect, where to focus our faith. Then it works in us the very faith it proclaims.

Charismatics understand the external Word in a dynamic, not a static, sense. They do not see the once-and-for-all character of the gospel as ruling out the ongoing revelation of the Spirit. Rather, it is the gospel itself which encourages us to expect ongoing revelation. Jesus did not say, 'Lo, the Scriptures will be with you ... Lo, my words will be with you ...' He said: "Lo! *I* am with you always, to the close of the age" (Matt. 28:20). The personal presence of the Lord, through the Holy Spirit, is the substance of our faith, and the ongoing expression of the gospel.[96] Where He, whom the external Word proclaims, is present, so also will the gifts and revelations of His Spirit come into manifestation.

CHAPTER TEN

Pastoral Guidelines

Charismatics testify to a renewal of their spiritual life. Many of them appear to have a new interest in prayer, Bible study, witnessing; they give more freely of their time and money.

The charismatic renewal, however, has not come without problems. While it has contributed to spiritual renewal in some congregations, in others it has caused upset and division. For some Lutherans, the theology and experience which they see in the charismatic movement appear alien to our Lutheran heritage.

Can the positive factors in the charismatic movement help bring renewal to our Lutheran congregations? Can the negative effects be avoided?

The answer to these questions hinges on one factor above all others: *wise pastoral care.* The charismatic renewal has raised significant theological issues. Theological clarification is a necessary aspect of the renewal. But more important, at the level of congregational life, is the effect of pastoral concern and guidance. Every movement of God requires effective pastoral oversight if it is to develop in a wholesome way.

The following guidelines are offered as a help for Lutheran pastors and congregations.

1. *Become informed.* Seek to obtain an accurate and balanced view of what is happening in the charismatic renewal. Discuss the matter with other pastors or laymen who have firsthand experience. Attend some charismatic prayer meetings. Take in a charismatic conference or festival.

The charismatic renewal is sometimes referred to under the category of a "movement." This designation can be helpful as we seek to understand and relate to it.

Using this designation we would view the charismatic movement as functionally parallel, say, to the liturgical movement or the social action movement. These movements have a concern to recall the church to certain things in its heritage which have been neglected.

When the liturgical movement talks about liturgy and worship, it is not staking out an exclusivist claim on the life of worship. On the contrary, it is saying that this is something the whole church ought to be doing, but it hasn't been doing it, at least not as well as it ought to. So the liturgical movement is waving a flag, telling the church something important about its worship life.

The charismatic movement is waving a flag to the church, saying there are things which have been neglected, things we would generally group under the Third Article of the Creed: the person, works, and gifts of the Holy Spirit. In waving this flag, charismatics have two things in mind—

(1) They are doing this in and for the whole church. Their ultimate goal is to see the "movement" fade out, as the message is received and integrated into the ongoing life of the church.

(2) The charismatic flag represents a specific and valid concern. It does not represent "the whole counsel of God." In order for the charismatic renewal to remain balanced, it wants to see its message set in the context of all that the church proclaims and teaches.

2. *Accept.* People who have had charismatic experiences need to feel that their concerns and their experiences are understood and accepted by their pastor and fellow members. Rejection or mere tolerance closes the door to effective pastoral ministry. In 1969, the American Bishops of the Roman Catholic Church issued a statement on the charismatic renewal which evidenced a warm and wholesome pastoral attitude:

> It must be admitted that theologically the Movement has legitimate reasons for existence. It has a strong biblical basis. It would be difficult to inhibit the working of the Spirit which manifested itself so abundantly in the early church. The participants in the movement claim that they receive certain charismatic gifts. Admittedly, there have been abuses, but the cure is not the denial of their existence but their proper use.
>
> Perhaps our most prudent way to judge the validity of the claims of the Movement is to observe the effects on those who participate in the prayer meetings. There are many indications that this participation leads to a better understanding of the role the Christian plays in the world. Many have experienced progress in their spiritual life.[97]

The pastor is usually the key to how the charismatic renewal will be received and used in the church. Whether a pastor himself personally becomes involved is a matter between himself and the Lord. But that he will need to give sound pastoral guidance in the matter is a virtual certainty. This movement of the Holy Spirit is widespread. Undoubtedly there has been much of it in which wisdom has been lacking. But it is real, and our people are coming into it in increasing numbers. The question is no longer, "Should we have this experience?" Our people are going to have it: In a prayer group, through listening to the testimony of a neighbor who has come into the experience, through reading about it—in one way or another—our people are receiving this experience. They need good pastoral guidance. There can be poor theology and undisciplined practice tied to a perfectly genuine experience. The pastor is called to shepherd his people in this matter just as he would in any other matter of the Faith.

One young girl received the gift of speaking in tongues, and her first thought was, "Oh, I must tell my pastor!" She was enthused, as only a teenager can be, and expected her pastor to share this joy. He remarked coldly, "Well, I don't suppose we can expel you from the church for this, but—" The impression he left was that she had done something almost serious enough to warrant expulsion from the church. The Bible tells us to "try the spirits"—not condemn them out of hand, on blind prejudice. The pastor who downgrades charismatic experience, to a parishioner who has been touched by it, misses a great opportunity to lead that person on in the things of God.

3. *Evaluate.* To accept a person and his experience does not mean that a pastor must accept the person's own theological description of that experience. Lutheran charismatics have sometimes described their experience in terms which are foreign to our heritage, i.e., the categories of classical Pentecostalism. With patience, this kind of problem can actually become the occasion for a deepened

appreciation of spiritual truth both for pastor and people. To accept the charismatic renewal, therefore, does not mean that one accepts a set of strange doctrines. Rather, one accepts a particular work of the Holy Spirit which is taking place in our time, and seeks to understand it and relate to it in a positive way.

Theologically, what the charismatic renewal brings to the church belongs to the inheritance of the church. Thus it brings nothing new to the church. What it does bring is an awareness that what she already has can be appropriated at a new level of experience. With this understanding, given patience and care, charismatic renewal can be experienced and interpreted within the framework of our Lutheran heritage and tradition.

4. *Take a positive, pastoral attitude.* Essentially the charismatic renewal is people; some of those involved are our people. There is no need for them to be lost to the Lutheran church. As we relate to them in a positive, pastoral way, the majority of them will respond with gratitude.

The statement of the Catholic bishops, mentioned above, concluded with these words:

> It is the conclusion of the committee on Doctrine that the movement should at this point not be inhibited but allowed to develop . . . Bishops must keep in mind their responsibility to oversee and guide this movement in the Church . . . In practice we recommend that Bishops involve prudent priests to be associated with this movement. Such involvement and guidance would be welcomed by charismatics.

A Lutheran charismatic one day approached his pastor and said, "You can't get off the hook on this charismatic thing. You are my spiritual authority." A week later the pastor met the man and said laconically, "I accept." It was the beginning of a warm pastoral relationship.

Many people who have had charismatic experience realize their need for spiritual authority. An experience may awaken a person to new potential in the Christian life, but it does not of itself mature one. Maturity comes through patient discipleship, which includes submission to those whom God sets over us. The lawless, independent spirit hinders the work of God. The pastor must be ready to accept the responsibility of guiding members who have had charismatic experiences.

When a congregation has a fair number of charismatics, a prayer group could be started within the congregation itself. This should be set under the leadership of a responsible person who would keep in regular touch with the pastor and leaders of the congregation. The pastor himself may want to assume leadership of the group. If the prayer group is publicly announced and is open to all who wish to attend, there need be no divisiveness. Indeed, its ministry of prayer and intercession can become a great blessing to the entire congregation.

When a congregation has only a few charismatics or when no one wishes to assume leadership of a prayer group, it may be that those interested could attend an ecumenical prayer group in the community with the knowledge and blessing of the pastor. They would, of course, be expected to maintain their loyalty and service to the congregation. In this kind of a situation, prayer groups which are identified with the Roman Catholic charismatic renewal will generally prove the most satisfactory because their theology of baptism and their interpretation of charismatic experience is more akin to our Lutheran tradition and heritage.

5. *Counsel patience.* Where differences or disagreements crop up in a congregation, precipitous action should be avoided. Both sides should be counseled to prayer and patience with the expectation that the Holy Spirit will bring unity. This will not necessarily mean uniformity, but, more likely, a deepened respect for one another and for the God-given variety of our experiences. Both those involved in the charismatic movement and those not involved need to learn to appreciate the gifts which the others have. And both need teaching to understand more fully how the charismatic renewal can help build up the life of the church.

6. *Maintain balance.* In the manifestation of charismatic gifts in the congregation, two extremes should be avoided: (1) undue emphasis upon any one gift; (2) suppression of any one gift. No gift of the Holy Spirit is without its special value, or God would not have set it in the church. When manifested in an orderly way, according to scriptural guidelines, each gift can bring its distinctive blessing to the body of Christ. The pastor must offer guidance and direction so that order and balance are maintained.

CHAPTER ELEVEN

Counsel for Lutheran Charismatics

Shortly after receiving the gift of tongues a Lutheran pastor was advised by David du Plessis: "Don't set your congregation on its ear. Move slowly. If your people fail to see in you the marks of love and humility, they will have every reason to doubt the authenticity of your experience." [98]

To bring new things to the church calls for a special exercise of wisdom and patience. The following suggestions are offered as a help to charismatics, both lay and clergy, as they seek to live out the implications of their charismatic experience within the Lutheran church.

1. Earn the right to be heard. Charismatics have sometimes been too quick to talk in detail and at length about their own experience. It is true, of course, that a moving experience fills one with enthusiasm; it is hard to keep it to yourself. But what you have to share carries more impact when it is backed up by positive fruit which others have had a chance to observe in your life. A group in Germany puts it this way: "Don't speak until you are asked. But live so that you will be asked." [99]

This does not mean that you should hide your

experience, or say nothing whatsoever about it. Rather, there needs to be a balance, the testimony of your actions as well as your words. Among those who already know you (family, congregation) the testimony of a changed life will have the greatest initial impact.

Many charismatics have shared with others their testimony and their enthusiasm only to see the other person turned off. Why is this? How can something so meaningful to you evoke a cool or even negative response in others?

Part of it may be simply this, you have depended too much on purely verbal communication. In order to communicate a deeply personal experience to someone else, you must first translate it into the language of love and service. A fellow church member who sees you repairing a broken window at church, or living well as a family, or becoming involved in the needs of the community is learning something about charismatic experience before you ever mention the word. The charismatic movement actually began when an Episcopal priest noticed that two of his members had begun tithing. When he asked about it, they shared with him their experience of renewal in the Holy Spirit. [100]

The following advice, to those who have received the gift of tongues, would apply in regard to charismatic experience generally:

1. Speaking in tongues does not make you a mature and seasoned Christian overnight. It is a *tool*, to be used faithfully in your daily prayers as one means of attaining to maturity. At first you may experience considerable joy and exuberance in the practice of the gift because it is new. Later, it will settle more into a quiet routine. This does not mean that you have 'lost something.' It just means that you have moved into the next phase; your 'new

tongue' is becoming second nature to you. Its purpose is not to give you a continual thrill, but rather to provide you with one more way—a wonderful, God-given way—for Christ to become formed in you.

2. Use this gift primarily in your private devotions. St. Paul says that one who speaks in tongues edifies *himself*. Speaking in tongues opens up a new dimension in personal prayer which can effect deep changes and blessings in your Christian life. For the most part this is not a gift to be displayed openly, but is a private language of adoration, praise, devotion, and intercession between you and God.

3. Be modest and quiet about your own experience. Some of the other members in the congregation may find charismatic experience hard to accept. Talk and argument will not help. This blessing cannot be forced on anyone, nor should any 'pressure' ever be applied. If an opportunity presents itself, share your testimony in a simple way— and then let the Lord use it in His own way with that individual.

4. Seek fellowship with others who share your joy and enthusiasm in this blessing. But guard against forming any 'cliques' within the congregation. Prayer meetings and group get-togethers should generally be open to any member of the congregation. Beware of spiritual pride. (See I Corinthians 4:7.)

5. Make certain that the testimony of your words is backed up by the testimony of your *life*. The most convincing evidence that you have truly received a blessing from the Lord is the effect which it comes to have in your everyday life. Be on hand when there is work to do in the congregation—humble, obscure tasks that need to be done, but which often get little recognition. Practical work is a necessary balance wheel in the spiritual life; you can't live on a solid diet of prayer meetings and Bible study. Furthermore, this is one of the most effective testimonies you can make in the congregation. Unconsciously your fellow members will say, "There must be something to it, all right. When there's a job to do, you can always count on them." [101]

Charismatics, in pursuing their new-found interests, have not always been attentive to letting the Spirit speak through them in these nonverbal ways. One Lutheran pastor, himself a charismatic, expressed some disappointment when he said: "When we have prayer meetings and Bible studies, the charismatics are right there. But when there's *work* to be done around the church, it's the old-line Lutherans I can count on."

Another danger in saying too much too soon is that you will tend to borrow interpretation and perspective from others. This is one of the things that happened in the early years of the charismatic renewal. Lutherans borrowed their interpretation of charismatic experience from classical Pentecostalism.

Allow time for the Lord to establish your walk in the Spirit, your relationships with fellow members, and your over-all understanding of charismatic renewal; this is the kind of wisdom and patience that earns you the right to be heard.

2. *"Judge not."* A common sin among charismatics is judging. "Our church is dead. . . . The pastor is not spiritual. . . . They don't have any interest in prayer or Bible study. . . . We don't get 'fed' there. . . . They're so negative about the Holy Spirit. . . ." This is the sin that Paul pointed out in Corinth, the sin of 'party spirit.' It flourished side by side with spiritual gifts and detracted from the effectiveness of the gifts.

Charismatic renewal should lead to a deepening of mutual esteem within the Body of Christ. This does not mean that there is no place for criticism and admonition. But in order for it to be constructive, there must first be established the feeling of unity. Judging proceeds from an "us/them" mentality,

Spirit-led admonition from a "we" mentality.

Charismatics have not always been sensitive to the hurt they have caused fellow Christians by even their best-intentioned criticisms. Your own testimony can come across as a giant put-down, if it carries the implication that anyone without a similar experience is a deficient or second-rate Christian.

3. Appreciate your heritage. The very word "renewal" implies an appreciation of the old. God is not an annihilator, He is a redeemer. He does not obliterate the old, He renews it. He does not make all new things, He makes all things new. A mark of maturity in any renewal movement is an appreciation of its heritage.

Kilian McDonnell warns against importing "cultural baggage" from one religious tradition to another.[102] By cultural baggage he means such things as style of worship, speech mannerisms, hymnody, theological and pastoral traditions.

Charismatics, for instance, have a maddening way of saying, "The Lord told me . . ." They talk like they have a private line to heaven. This is not the way Lutherans traditionally speak of their communications with God.

A Lutheran seminary professor once pursued this issue with a charismatic pastor whom he was visiting. The evening the professor arrived they had talked about a call which the pastor had received to serve in another parish. The following morning the pastor announced at breakfast, "The Lord told me to accept the call."

"What exactly do you mean?" the professor asked. "Did He speak to you in an audible voice?"

"Oh, no . . ."

"What then? Was it some kind of unusual experience?"

"Not really. It's just that I know He wants me to take the call."

"You prayed about it?"

"Yes."

"And you came to the conviction that God was leading you to accept?"

"That's right."

"Well, why didn't you say so?" [103]

Well, he *did* say so. But he did it in Pentecostal idiom, which is one way, but not the only way, to describe the working of the Spirit. And not always the most effective in a Lutheran setting.

Certainly different cultures can be enriched by interaction with one another. One may recognize, for instance, a wonderful presence of the Spirit in a free, exuberant Pentecostal worship service. That does not mean that Lutherans should adopt a Pentecostal worship style. Mere imitation does not bring renewal. Interaction between different cultures and traditions should lead both groups to seek the Lord with new urgency. It is His plan for our renewal, not imitation of other renewed groups, which should be the focus of our hope and expectation.

How can you relate to your Lutheran heritage in a positive way? One practical way is to seek the ministry of your church in the areas of its strength, not at a point of weakness.

Your pastor or congregation may have had little or no experience with the kind of free praise that goes on in a charismatic prayer meeting; healing, speaking in tongues, and prophecy may be unexplored areas. If you come fresh from your charismatic experience expecting that this kind of interest and ministry will shortly be kindled in your congregation, you will be disappointed and those you come to may become frustrated or angry.

What are the strengths of your pastor? Perhaps

he is a strong teacher, or an able counselor. Seek out his ministry at a point where God has especially gifted him. He may fill in areas not touched by your charismatic experience.

What are the strengths of your congregation, or your Lutheran tradition? The fact that much of it may have been "dead form" before your charismatic experience probably says as much about you as about your church. One thing that renewal in the Holy Spirit does is open your eyes to see reality and truth where you didn't see it before. What treasures are waiting to be mined in the teaching and theological heritage of the Lutheran church, in its hymns, in its regard for Word and Sacrament?

4. Live under the cross. The strength of the charismatic renewal is its lively sense of expectation. The expectation has a precise focus: Charismatics expect the intervention of God in everyday life.

In order for this to be operative, one must live continually in the shadow of the cross. Charismatic living is not something *we* do. It is, again, and again, God bringing us to the point of helplessness, where *He* acts. It is death to self.

Charismatics do not always recognize this at first. They are caught up in a sense of the glory and power of God. Later, there is no way of avoiding the cross, because the Spirit himself presses it home. Father Tom Forest, a leader in the Roman Catholic charismatic renewal in Puerto Rico, made the point that "only the beginning is 'magical.' As you grow, it gets harder. The gifts are a humiliation because they take you beyond yourself; God himself is at work. The gifts are a calling to service. The bigger the gift the greater the crucifixion to service." [104]

The life of holiness bears the same mark. It is not the result of my pious striving but of God's gracious intervention.

Christian growth refers to the growth of the Spirit's work in our lives. The Spirit grows and moves forward. We die and move backwards, Christ lives, we die. That's Christian growth. [105]

To live under the cross means to despair of one's own power and effort, and at the same time to trust mightily in the power of God. This is true in regard to receiving forgiveness of sins. It is true in the manifestation of spiritual gifts. It is true in the exercise of love. It characterizes the Christian life from beginning to end. Charismatic renewal is a new pilgrimage to Calvary.

CHAPTER TWELVE

Charismatic Renewal and the Lutheran Church

What is the charismatic renewal saying to the Lutheran church about its congregational life, about the quality of its fellowship in the Spirit?

What follows is a positive picture, based on a variety of contacts and firsthand experience. Its purpose is to highlight some of the questions and challenges which the charismatic renewal is posing to the Lutheran church.

Worship. Charismatic renewal has vitalized worship. For many people, what had been routine has been transformed into a dynamic, joyful, Spirit-given encounter with God and with fellow believers.

The most typical expression has been the prayer meeting. Largely informal and spontaneous, it brings together such elements as singing (the renewal has already produced a significant hymnody), testimony, prophecy, teaching, prayers for healing, prayers for personal needs (often accompanied by the laying on of hands), and of course, much free prayer, including speaking or singing in tongues.

In some Lutheran, Anglican, and Catholic circles the renewal has influenced liturgical worship

as well. The structure of the service may be opened
up to allow for more spontaneous or participatory
expressions. For instance, the reading of Scripture
may be followed by a time of free prayer; the distri-
bution of communion may be accompanied by words
of prophecy; the sermon may make room for response and testimony from the congregation; verbal
intercessions may be augmented by direct ministry with laying-on-of-hands. Where a congregation
has two services, one may be opened up for this
kind of innovation, while the other retains a more
familiar format, for members who prefer a more
traditional mode of worship.

The form of charismatic worship is not as important as that which gives rise to it: a sense of
expectancy. People expect God to speak and act
among them—not only through the pastor or the formal worship structure, but through a many-mem-
bered, variously gifted Body.

What is the state of the prayer life, private and
corporate, in our Lutheran congregations? How vital
is the worship service in a Lutheran congregation
on a typical Sunday morning? Is the church ready
to receive this impulse from the charismatic renewal
for a more vital experience of worship?

Bible. Renewed and deepened interest in the Bible is a basic ingredient of the charismatic renewal.

One aspect of this is broad, and is not unique
to the charismatic renewal; it is, nevertheless, an
important part of what is going on in the renewal.
This broad interest is not focused on any particular
part of the Bible. At a charismatic prayer meeting
or conference virtually any part of the Bible could
turn up as subject for the Bible study. Charismatics
have a great interest in studying the Bible. They
recognize it as authoritative for Christian faith and

life and are eager to increase their understanding of it.

Charismatics rarely have to be exhorted to read their Bibles. The raw material of enthusiasm is there. They are eager to be taught. Is the church prepared to capitalize on this readiness? Have the pastors and teachers of the church made the necessary effort to gain their trust and confidence?

The charismatic renewal has a second, more specialized interest in the Bible. Their experience of the Holy Spirit and His gifts is linked to Scripture in a twofold way: On the one hand charismatics find in the Bible the source of their expectations; they expect the gifts and power of the Spirit to be operative in their lives because these things are promised in Scripture. On the other hand, charismatic experience is very much subjected to the tests and norms of Scripture; it is not spiritual experiences and phenomena as such which gain a standing in the charismatic renewal, but rather that which is understood, on the basis of Scripture, to be a manifestation of the Holy Spirit. (A practical illustration of this would be seen in the suspicion with which charismatics regard such things as healings, visions, or revelations which are associated with the realm of the psychic or occult. Not that charismatics would dismiss the possibility or reality of such phenomena, but they would judge them to be alien and opposed to valid Christian experience.)

This special interest in the charismatic phenomena in Scripture does not lead to a new set of doctrines or new methods of interpreting Scripture. What it does is open up possibilities of understanding the text in new ways. For example, because things like healings, visions, exorcisms, tongue speaking and interpretation occur in their own midst, charismatics find little difficulty in accepting the biblical record of such happenings as historically accurate. This does not make them "wooden literalists" in their approach to Scripture. Charismatics with background and training in Scripture interpretation do not abandon the scholarly study of Scripture when they become charismatic. Rather, they bring new kinds of questions to the text.

This may be one of the ways in which the charismatic renewal is offering a fresh impetus to biblical studies in the Lutheran church.

Evaluating the Renewal. A careful reading of charismatic literature reveals that already in this young movement there are self-critical and evaluative forces at work. This is even more evident when one participates in charismatic conferences and consultations at the leadership level. Both the theology and practices taking place within the renewal come in for searching evaluation. Speaking at a theological consultation on the Doctrine of the Holy Spirit, Lutheran theologian Richard Jensen said, "The kind of self-criticism that goes on in the charismatic renewal is more rigorous than anything I have seen in the Lutheran church itself." Is the Lutheran church at this point being challenged to remember her task of "continual self-reformation"?

Beyond the self-critical task, "church" and "renewal movement" can be further helped as they submit to evaluation by one another.

The charismatic renewal has brought people into certain kinds of experience, for example, renewal of prayer, the exercise of certain spiritual gifts such as tongues, prophecy, vision, etc., ecumenical fellowships and communities. These need evaluation from points-of-view outside as well as within the movement. Lutheran charismatics would profit by testing the insights and the experience growing out of the renewal against the wisdom and experience of the church, especially the historic Lutheran norms of Scripture and the Lutheran confessions.

Within traditional church structures people likewise are brought into a variety of experiences, for example, disciplined worship and church membership, systematic theological work, catechetical instruction, social involvement. These, also, need the kind of evaluation which could come from the charismatic renewal.

The habits and practices of the church are brought under scrutiny by any renewal movement. Is the church ready to receive this kind of scrutiny from the charismatic movement?

Order and Authority. In the charismatic movement a fairly widespread emphasis on order and authority has emerged. Critics fault charismatics for constructing a whole spirituality around private experience. Yet a cavalier spiritual individualism is more challenged in the milieu of the charismatic renewal than in the average Lutheran congregation. Charismatics see personal experience and behavior as subject to structures of authority.

This has come about through a serious examination of family and church order. Generally speaking, hierarchical as opposed to egalitarian or democratic models have prevailed. Charismatics speak easily and without embarrassment of father-led families, elder-led communities.

Charismatics are doing more than theorizing about the structure of Christian community. They are putting their insights to hard tests of practice. They are shaping their understanding of words like "authority," "submission," "headship," "responsibility," "obedience," and "freedom" in the context of radically committed relationships. Where this kind of emphasis has taken root and had a chance to mature, forms of Christian fellowship and community have developed which can be instructive for a greater understanding of inter-personal relationships.

An age widely characterized by an anti-authority mood and militant individualism is being offered by the charismatic movement some serious counter-proposals. These proposals speak both to the culture at large and to the church. Is the church open to consider the proposals, even though they run counter to some popular currents of the day? Is she prepared to call into question her tendency simply to go along with what is fashionable?

Those involved in the charismatic renewal do not fancy that they have some kind of unique experience or authority in virtue of which they are to call the church into judgment. Their experience may have helped them formulate the questions, but their right to speak them is the right of any believer to raise questions which the church should consider. And the questions are raised for the healing and upbuilding of the church.

Throughout this book we have referred to the charismatic *renewal*. Can a movement arrogate to itself the call or the claim to renew the church? I do not believe so. Renewal, in a sense, is a by-product—a by-product of *truth*. This movement among God's people offers hope for the renewal of the church simply and only because it bears witness to the truth. With all its weaknesses and failings, I believe that it has laid hold upon essential truth, and it is participation in this truth that I covet for the Lutheran church.

CHAPTER THIRTEEN

Lutheran Charismatic Renewal Services

Someone has quipped, "God so loved the world that He did not send a committee." Our human tendency to over-organize can stifle the free working of the Spirit.

One of the things we have learned, however, is that a movement of the Spirit needs a certain minimum of structure if it is to continue. The "Jesus Revolution" of the 1960s was short-lived as a widespread movement because it produced virtually no structure. In the early 1970s it became evident to a number of leaders that the charismatic renewal among Lutherans needed some kind of structure, a focal point of visibility, in order to present a sustained and credible witness both to the Lutheran church and ecumenically on behalf of the Lutheran tradition.

Several structures had begun to develop independently, simply out of need. In 1972 an International Lutheran Conference on the Holy Spirit was held in Minneapolis which drew more than 10,000 people. This became an annual event, each year increasing in attendance.

In 1974 and 1975 National Leaders' Conferences were held in Ann Arbor, Michigan, drawing together about 250 leaders in Lutheran charismatic renewal from the United States and Canada.

In addition to these conferences, a number of independent charismatic Lutheran ministries have grown up since the mid-1960s.

Beginning in the fall of 1973 these various groups and ministries began to be drawn together. It was evident that the Lord had been forming leaders among the Lutherans, and that the time was right for them to begin working more closely together. Over the period of the next 18 months a simple structure emerged. Lutheran Charismatic Renewal Services (LCRS) was formed as a vehicle to serve and coordinate the various aspects of charismatic renewal among Lutherans.

The Service Committee of LCRS consists of leaders, both clergy and laity, who have been drawn together in the work of the renewal, and are able to devote a certain amount of extra time to serving in this way. The structure is open-ended, so people can be added to the Service Committee, or leave it, as needs and situations change.

More important than the structure were the personal ties which began to be formed between leaders. Men who had known each other in varying degrees over the previous decade began to work together more closely. The variety of their gifts and ministries were brought to more precise focus in the service of the renewal. In the Service Committee, in clusters of regional and local leadership, and in independent ministries a greater sense of Lutheran identity and cohesiveness began to take shape. Men sensed themselves being knit together not only to accomplish a task, but to illustrate in a visible way the unity which the Lord desired in the renewal and in the church.

This did not come about easily or at once. Indeed, the process continues. Men who had operated more-

or-less independently began to consult with one another, submit their own plans to the judgment of brethren. We learned what it meant to wrestle through disagreements and misunderstandings. Out of it emerged a heightened trust and regard for one another, a deeper unity in the Lord. LCRS, and the various segments of the renewal which it serves, is more than an organizational structure. It is a network of relationships which is being forged together on the Lord's anvil as an earnest of His work in the renewal as a whole.

By the time of the Third International Lutheran Conference on the Holy Spirit in the summer of 1974, this work among the leaders was beginning to spread. "The obvious unity among the leaders, and the effect this had upon the participants, was the most noteworthy aspect of the entire conference," said an official observer from The American Lutheran Church, in his evaluation of the 1974 Conference.

A member of the Church Council of the ALC wrote: "I am grateful for the quality of leadership that has surfaced among the Lutherans in the charismatic movement. Closely related to this is the direction your leaders are giving to this movement.

"In some of the workshops I attended, and especially in the two final general sessions of the Conference, there was a very clear message to the audience for them to remain loyal and faithful to their respective local congregations and their synodical leaders. This I deeply appreciate.

"For meaningful dialogue and constructive co-operation to prevail between the synodical bodies and the charismatic movement, there must be a cadre of leaders who can speak for the Lutheran charismatics.

"Part of the thrust of this letter is to encourage

the leaders of this movement to forcefully assume their leadership role. I would like to see you take more initiative in entering into dialogue with the bishops and other synodical leaders."

A theological professor, in making his report, had this to say about the Lutheran charismatic leaders. "It is a leadership that wants to be responsible. They are by no means schismatics.

"I have a good deal of confidence in these men. It is a new leadership and it is good leadership. These are men with whom the church and the seminaries may easily enter into dialogue. I think it would be true to say that the most helpful sign I saw (at the Conference) was the direction in which this new leadership is moving.

"We must keep in contact with these men. They are open to dialogue with us, very open. Are we as open to them?" [106]

"We have come a country mile since last year in strengthening the leadership of the renewal," said Rodney Lensch in the closing message of the 1974 Conference. "There is a solidarity and unity among the brethren. It is a miracle of God.

"The Lutheran public and the public at large are seeing what the Lord is doing in the land. It is clear that the charismatic movement is here to stay, and Lutherans are deeply involved in it."

LCRS serves a threefold function. It recognizes, first of all, a shepherding responsibility for Lutheran charismatics. It seeks to provide help and resources for those involved in the renewal, through such things as conferences, tapes, information and literature, assistance to local leaders. Without much clanking of machinery, Lutherans involved in the renewal are being strengthened in a variety of ways for witness and service.

Secondly, LCRS serves as a necessary point-of-contact between church officials and the renewal. It is difficult for the institutional church to relate to a widespread, unstructured movement. LCRS seeks to maintain communication and good relationships with Lutheran church officials and to communicate their concerns to those involved in the renewal.

A number of Lutheran charismatics, both clergy and laity, are presently living or serving outside the formal structures of the Lutheran church. Some have made this choice themselves, some have been forced or frozen out of the Lutheran church because the church would not accept their charismatic experience and witness.

A third task of LCRS is to relate to these individuals and groups who are outside the structure, and to represent their concerns to the church. Many of them still maintain a keen sense of their Lutheran identity. In any honest appraisal they must be recognized as an important part of the charismatic renewal among Lutherans. Insofar as some have been dealt with unfairly, or have acted unwisely, and the possibility of reconciliation remains, they represent unfinished business for the church and for the renewal.

From the beginning, the charismatic renewal has had a strong ecumenical thrust. The ecumenical involvement has not been organizational, neither has it been superficial. It has been at the level of a common experience of the reality of the Spirit and the acknowledgment of the lordship of Christ. Denominational differences have not been wiped away, but a deep-felt sense of unity—one could almost say an obligation of unity—has continued to hover over the renewal. Seasoned observers of the ecumenical movement have singled out the charismatic renewal as the most vital and significant thing happening in the ecumenical scene today. [107] LCRS maintains close ties with leaders representing other sectors of the charismatic renewal, recognizing that we have a distinctive contribution to make as Lutherans, and also have much to gain from Christians of other traditions and backgrounds.

LCRS came into being in response to a need—the need for Lutheran charismatics to draw closer together, to gain a deepened sense of their own identity, to present a more effective witness to their own church, and at the same time to share fully in the great renewing work which the Holy Spirit is doing throughout the whole church. It is, as its name implies, a service body. "Our only authority," said Steve Clark, speaking of the Service Committee for the Catholic Charismatic Renewal, "derives from a job well done. If we serve well, in planning a conference or supplying some other need, we may be called on again."

LCRS is there for just that purpose—to be called on, to serve.

CHAPTER FOURTEEN

Further Reading

St. Paul began his instruction to the Corinthian charismatics by saying, "I do not want you to be uninformed" (1 Cor. 12:1). Many of the problems in the charismatic renewal are the by-product of ignorance. A basic requirement for those involved in charismatic renewal, or interested in it, is to become informed.

The presses are pouring out charismatic literature at an astonishing rate. Before the ink has dried on this page, the bibliography given below will be dated. Nevertheless, we felt it would be good to point our readers to some materials of proven worth, which can add to one's understanding of charismatic renewal, its significance for the individual and for the church. These works are not necessarily Lutheran in their slant, nor would we endorse everything that is presented. We have found these works to be generally helpful, but the reader must exercise judgment as to what he accepts and applies.

Introduction to Charismatic Renewal

Popular Testimonies

The Gift Is Already Yours by Erwin Prange. A Lutheran pastor's story of his personal journey into the joy and power of charismatic renewal, told with wit and candor. Along the way he offers helpful interpretation as to the significance of charismatic experience in the life of a congregation. (Logos International, Plainfield, N.J., 1973, 150 pages, $2.95.)

The Cross and the Switchblade by David Wilkerson. The story of a young Pentecostal preacher who goes into the slums of New York to work with teenage gangs, finds that miracles happen when they open themselves up to the word of the gospel, and the power of the Holy Spirit. Exciting reading. Good to give out to people who are more likely to be reached through a story than through direct teaching. (Spire Books, Old Tappan, N.J., 1963, 173 pages, 75¢.)

Aglow with the Spirit by Robert Frost. A college professor tells how the Holy Spirit transformed both his personal and his academic life. Interspersed in the story is helpful instructional material on the nature of charismatic experience. (Logos International, Plainfield, N.J., 1965, 126 pages, $1.25.)

Nine O'Clock in the Morning by Dennis Bennett. It was the outbreak of charismatic experience in the author's Episcopal parish in Van Nuys, California, in 1960, that sparked the modern charismatic movement. Here he tells his personal story, perhaps the most influential testimony in the movement to date. A close, honest look at a charismatic pioneer, who shares both the joys and the struggles of walking in the Spirit. (Logos International, Plainfield, N.J., 1970, 209 pages, $2.50.)

They Speak with Other Tongues by John Sherrill. The testimony of a professional journalist who came to jeer and stayed to pray. Step by step he tells how his research into the charismatic movement became a personal quest, ending with his own experience of baptism with the Holy Spirit. An excellent introductory book, popularly written. (Spire Books, Old Tappan, N.J., 1964, 143 pages, 95¢.)

Historical Surveys

As At the Beginning by Michael Harper. A popular historical survey of the beginnings of the charismatic renewal, from the perspective of an Englishman. (Logos International, Plainfield, N.J., 1965, 128 pages, $1.25.)

Bold in the Spirit by Erling Jorstad. A history of the charismatic movement within Lutheran circles in the United States. Case studies of the way the renewal has worked in different situations. Personal testimonies. A summary of the most frequently raised criticisms of charismatic renewal, and some answers the author has found useful in speaking both to critics and supporters of the movement. (Augsburg, Minneapolis, 1974, 128 pages, $2.95.)

Instruction

Filled with New Wine by James Jones. One of the best studies of the charismatic renewal in the mainline churches, written in a scholarly yet popular vein. The author considers the history and theology of the renewal, addresses himself to the critics and to the dangers of the renewal. He is especially sympathetic to the sacramental point-of-view, and therefore the book is excellent for Lutherans. Probably the best and most balanced introduction to the renewal written so far. (Harper & Row, New York, 1974, 141 pages, $4.95.)

Speaking in Tongues and Its Significance for the Church by Larry Christenson. An explanation of speaking in tongues based on Scripture, theology, and personal experience. The first major study of the subject to come out of the charismatic movement, and the most widely distributed. Helpful for those who have questions, who are personally interested in the gift, or have recently received it. (Bethany Fellowship, Inc., Minneapolis, 1968, 141 pages, $1.25.)

The Gift of Tongues by Larry Christenson. An abbreviated treatment of the above title, in booklet form. Good for handing to someone who wants a condensed summary of the main questions which arise in connection with this gift. (Bethany Fellowship, Inc., Minneapolis, 1963, 32 pages, 25¢.)

Baptized in the Spirit by Stephen Clark. A widely respected leader in the charismatic renewal explains baptism in the Spirit from a Roman Catholic perspective. Balanced and practical. Generally helpful for Lutherans. (Dove Publications, Pecos, N.M., 1970, 50¢.)

What About Baptism? by Larry Christenson. The material from Chapter 7 of the present book in booklet form. Good to hand out to people who have questions about how charismatic renewal relates to the Lutheran practice of baptism. (Bethany Fellowship, Inc., Minneapolis, 1973, 23 pages, 25¢.)

Growing in the Spirit

Prayer

With Christ in the School of Prayer by Andrew Murray. A classic that leads you into a deeper and more disciplined prayer life. A month of daily readings, dealing with the fundamentals of effective prayer. (Spire Books, Old Tappan, N.J., 1953, 192 pages, 75¢.)

Hungry for God by Ralph Martin. A simple and practical examination of the role of prayer in the life of the committed Christian. Specific helps for developing a disciplined and effective prayer life, backed up with personal experience and illustration, by one of the outstanding leaders in the Catholic Charismatic Renewal. (Doubleday, New York, 1974, 168 pages, $5.95.)

Realities by Basilea Schlink. The founder of the Evangelical Sisterhood of Mary, Darmstadt, Germany, recounts the stories of answered prayer experienced during the early days of their sisterhood. Short chapters, engagingly written. Faith building. (Zondervan, Grand Rapids, 1966, 140 pages, $1.25.)

Healing

The Healing Light by Agnes Sanford. One of the first and the most influential books on prayer and healing that grew out of the healing movement in the Episcopal church. Practical, down-to-earth suggestions for developing a more effective prayer life, especially for praying "the prayer of faith" for the sick. (Logos International, Plainfield, N.J., 1947, 152 pages, $1.25.)

Healing by Francis MacNutt. The foremost authority on healing in the Catholic Charismatic Movement presents a clearly reasoned case for the healing ministry of the church. Rooted in Scripture and in a breadth of personal experience. Evidences a keen appreciation of the sacramental life of the church and its implications for healing. (Ave Maria Press, Notre Dame, 1974, 333 pages, $3.50.)

Deeper Life

Let Us Praise by Judson Cornwall. One of the most necessary and least understood aspects of prayer is presented in a graphic way. Practical helps for developing the art of praise, both privately and corporately. (Logos International, Plainfield, N.J., 1973, 148 pages, $2.95.)

The Renewed Mind by Larry Christenson. The idea behind this book is that Christian growth is by grace—a work of God in us, not something we do for God. The unique feature of the book is the idea that the renewed mind responds more to parables and images than to abstract principles. It presents a series of images and parables which can serve as practical handles for making principles working realities in everyday life. (Bethany Fellowship, Inc., Minneapolis, 1974, 127 pages, $2.45.)

Disciple by Juan Carlos Ortiz. Some traditional patterns for personal and congregational life are called in for critical examination. The author points out that "accepting Jesus as your Savior" is not the New Testament pattern, but rather coming under His lordship. A stirring challenge to commitment—both to Christ and to the Christian fellowship. (Creation House, Carol Stream, Ill., 1975, 158 pages, $1.75.)

The Christian's Secret of a Happy Life by Hannah W. Smith. The holiness classic, still going strong a hundred years later. Practical instruction aimed at "reckoning ourselves dead to sin and alive to God." Good for group or individual study. Has an excellent chapter on guidance. (Spire Books, Old Tappan, N.J., 1942, 174 pages, 95¢.)

The Normal Christian Life by Watchman Nee. The author is a popular resource in evangelical and charismatic circles. This book is a good sample of his thought. It is a study of Romans 5-8. Many helpful insights on developing the life of personal holiness. (Christian Literature Crusade, Ft. Washington, Pa., 1957, 192 pages, $1.50.)

Pastoral and Theological Orientation

Historical Works

The Holiness-Pentecostal Movement in the United States by Vinson Synan. The best popular history of the movements which were the forerunners of the modern day charismatic movement. Well researched, authoritative. Helpful for understanding some of the background, theology, and terminology which have had an influence on the charismatic movement. (Wm. B. Eerdmans, Grand Rapids, 1971, 248 pages, $5.95.)

The Pentecostals by Walter Hollenweger. The most comprehensive resource on the worldwide Pentecostal movement—its history, theology, and denominational make-up. The author also includes sections on the early development of the charismatic movement. (Augsburg, Minneapolis, 1972, 572 pages, $9.95.)

Biblical Works

Gifts and Graces, Gifts and Ministries by Arnold Bittlinger. These two books, by one of the most prolific and thoughtful Lutheran writers in Germany, provide some of the best biblical material available, from a charismatic viewpoint. The first book is a commentary on 1 Corinthians 12-14. The second is an exposition of the New Testament teaching on ministry. Scholarly, yet simply and understandably written. Excellent resource for pastors and leaders. (Wm. B. Eerdmans, Grand Rapids, 1973, about 110 pages each, $1.95 each.)

These are Not Drunken As You Suppose by Howard Ervine. A professor of New Testament builds a scriptural case for charismatic renewal. He considers the texts (starting with Matthew, then digging into Acts and 1 Corinthians), takes up the standard criticisms, deals with the conflicting exegeses. He adds helpful background for understanding the situation in the church at Corinth. His interpretation is somewhat closer to classical Pentecostalism than is true of Lutherans or Catholics. (Logos International, Plainfield, N.J., 1968, 241 pages, $2.50.)

Interpretation of Charismatic Renewal

A New Pentecost by Leon Joseph Cardinal Suenens. A positive evaluation of the charismatic renewal by one of the leading cardinals of the Roman Catholic Church. He examines the role of the Holy Spirit in the church from earliest times as a background for understanding the current renewal. Helpful insights on the place of baptism, the laying on of hands, speaking in tongues. Even though the book is written for a Catholic audience (e.g., one chapter deals with the place of Mary in Catholic piety), the great majority of the book is a valuable resource for anyone seeking a balanced understanding of the charismatic renewal. (The Seabury Press, New York, 1974, 239 pages, $7.95.)

A Message to the Charismatic Movement by Larry Christenson. This study of a little-known charismatic awakening in 19th-century England offers an historical perspective for evaluating the charismatic renewal. The experience and teachings of the Catholic Apostolic Church are considered in terms of their value for the church today. Key topics include, "The Church: The Body of Christ," "The Baptism with the Holy Spirit," "Unity in the Body of Christ," "Ministry in the Body of Christ," and "Authority in the Body of Christ." (Bethany Fellowship, Inc., Minneapolis, 1972, 119 pages, $1.25.)

Unless the Lord Build the House by Ralph Martin. An early Catholic statement on the importance of the charismatic renewal for the church. Strong emphasis on the need to bring people to a solid commitment to Jesus as Lord and Savior, before they can be enlisted in projects of social action. Emphasizes the need for authentic Christian community. (Ave Maria Press, Notre Dame, 1971, 63 pages, 75¢.)

The Charismatic Movement in the Lutheran Church in America. This is the most helpful official statement by a Lutheran body which has been produced to date. Sub-titled "A Pastoral Perspective," it offers suggestions on how a Lutheran congregation can relate to the charismatic renewal. Evaluation of the renewal is basically positive and balanced. Suggestions for group study are included. (Board of Publications, LCA, 1974, 21 pages, 75¢.)

The Malines Document, "Theological and Pastoral Orientations on the Catholic Charismatic Renewal." This document is the result of a consultation of international leaders of the Catholic charismatic renewal who met under the sponsorship of Cardinal Suenens in Malines, Belgium, in 1974. It examines the theological basis of the renewal, the pastoral implications of the charisms, the use of terms like "baptized in the Spirit" and "charismatic." It has found wide acceptance not only in Catholic circles, but throughout the renewal. The sacramental viewpoint makes it generally helpful for Lutherans. One of the most balanced and helpful documents for an overall evaluation of the renewal. (Word of Life, Drawer A, Notre Dame, 1974, 71 pages, $2.00.)

The Work of the Holy Spirit. Report of the Special Committee on the Work of the Holy Spirit to the 182nd General Assembly of the United Presbyterian Church. This is one of the first official church studies which came out in a positive way on charismatic renewal. Good theological and practical guidelines for relating the renewal of the life of the church. The theological position is generally one which Lutherans can identify with. (Office of the General Assembly, 510 Witherspoon Building, Philadelphia, 1970, 56 pages, 75¢.)

Catholic Pentecostalism: Problems in Evaluation by Kilian McDonnell. This is one of the first works which presented a positive evaluation of the renewal by a competent theologian who had done extensive firsthand research of the movement. He explodes some of the stereotypes, such as the idea that Pentecostals and charismatics are socially and culturally backward, that tongues is the center of the whole movement, that the renewal is largely based on emotion. He also calls for more competent exegetical and theological work within the renewal itself. (Dove Publications, Pecos, N.M., 1970, 58 pages, 50¢.)

Era of the Spirit by J. Rodman Williams. A Presbyterian theologian draws out some of the theological implications of the charismatic renewal, relating it to traditional categories of theology such as faith, assurance, sanctification. In the second part of the book he takes up the teaching on the Holy Spirit in four well-known theologians: Barth, Brunner, Tillich, and Bultmann; he sees in their writings a foreshadowing of many of the things which are happening in the charismatic renewal. (Logos International, Plainfield, N.J., 1971, 110 pages, $1.95.)

Encounter with God by Morton Kelsey. While this book does not deal directly with charismatic renewal, it provides a philosophical and theological framework for better understanding the renewal. Its essential value is that of providing an intellectual framework or rationale for many of the experiences which people are having, such as prophecy, vision, healing, tongues, etc. Scholarly and well-researched. Worthwhile reading for pastors and teachers. (Bethany Fellowship, Inc., Minneapolis, 1972, 281 pages, $5.95.)

Social Action—Jesus Style by Larry Christenson. A paperback revision of the book titled *A Charismatic Approach to Social Action.* Some of the inadequacies of a non-involved evangelicalism and a nonbiblical social activism are examined against the background of social concern which is developing in the charismatic renewal. Two elements which offer a fresh approach are highlighted: a greater experience of guidance in determining where and how to become involved, and the growth of Christian communities as a more effective instrument for social action. (Bethany Fellowship, Inc.,

Minneapolis, 1974, 112 pages, $1.25.)

The Charismatic Church by William Olson. A Lutheran chaplain makes a theological and practical evaluation of the charismatic renewal, using several "case studies" to pinpoint his arguments. Against this background he makes a strong case for relating the renewal to the life of the congregation. Persuasive and straightforward. (Bethany Fellowship, Inc., Minneapolis, 1974, 152 pages, $2.45.)

Where Are We Headed? by Stephen Clark. One of the outstanding lay leaders in the Catholic Charismatic Renewal takes a long-range look at where the renewal is—or ought to be—heading. The book consists of a series of practical guidelines for leaders who have a responsibility for shaping and guiding the renewal. Whereas it is written specifically for Catholic leaders, many of the points have equal application in a Lutheran setting. (CRS, Box 12, Notre Dame, 1973, 80 pages, $1.25.)

Spiritus Creator by Regin Prenter. While this book has no connection with the charismatic renewal, it is an important book for Lutherans: It is *a study of Luther's concept of the Holy Spirit.* The author shows how central to all Luther's thought was the person and work of the Holy Spirit. Scholarly, well-researched, provocative. Not easy reading, but well worth the effort. For pastors and theologians. (Fortress Press, Philadelphia, 1953, 311 pages, $1.90, paper.)

Periodicals

Lutheran Charismatic Renewal Newsletter. Box 14344, University Station, Minneapolis, Minnesota 55414. Sent free of charge to anyone requesting it. A monthly publication for Lutherans interested in charismatic renewal. Each issue contains a popular teaching article, and up-to-date news on the development of charismatic renewal among Lutherans.

New Covenant, Box 102, Ann Arbor, Michigan 48107, $5.00 per year. A monthly magazine serving the worldwide charismatic renewal. Excellent news coverage and teaching articles. The theological point-of-view is sacra-

mental and church-oriented, yet outspokenly charismatic. Significant input from the Catholic Charismatic
Renewal. For overall balance and growth, Lutherans
interested in charismatic renewal will certainly want
to subscribe.

New Wine, 264 S.W. 31st Street, Ft. Lauderdale, Florida
33315. Sent free of charge to anyone requesting it.
A high-quality magazine dedicated to Christian growth.
Many fine teaching articles. The writers are generally
from the Pentecostal or free church tradition, so the
theological position on some issues may be different
than Lutheran teaching. Nevertheless, the magazine
presents outstanding articles on many phases of the
Christian life, from a charismatic perspective, and is
well worth reading.

NOTES

1. See, for example, the "Lutheran Statement" in *New Wine Magazine,* February 1976, p. 2. Or articles in *New Covenant* presenting the distinctive Lutheran witness being made in the charismatic renewal, October 1973, April 1974, August 1974.
2. Jorstad, Erling. *Bold in the Spirit,* Augsburg Publishing House, Minneapolis, 1974, pp. 22-32.
3. *Kirche und Charisma,* Oekumenischer Verlag Dr. R. F. Edel, Marburg an der Lahn, Germany, p. 163. See also: Hollenweger, W. J. *The Pentecostals,* Augsburg Publishing House, Minneapolis, Minnesota, 1972, p. 246.
4. The author has had extensive firsthand contact and correspondence with Lutherans involved in charismatic renewal in all of these areas.
5. Strommen, Merton, P. et. al. *A Study of Generations,* Augsburg Publishing House, 1972, p. 119.
6. Clark, Stephen. *Where Are We Headed?* Charismatic Renewal Services, Box 12, Notre Dame, Indiana, 1973, pp. 8-13.
7. *Lutherans, the Spirit, the Gifts, and the Word,* unpublished manuscript edited by group of Missouri-Lutheran pastors, June 1973, pp. 8-13.
8. Brunner, Emil. *The Misunderstanding of the Church,* Lutterworth Press, London, 1952, pp. 49-52.
9. Muehlin, Heribert. In private conversation.
10. Williams, J. Rodman. *The Pentecostal Reality,* Logos International, Plainfield, N.J., 1972, footnote p. 19.
11. "Dialogue between the Secretariat for Promoting Christian Unity of the Roman Catholic Church and Leaders of some Pentecostal Churches and Participants in the Charismatic Movement within Protestant and Anglican Churches," Venice, Italy, May 21-26, 1975. From official Press Release.

12. Arndt, W. F. and Gingrich, F. W. *A Greek-English Lexicon of the New Testament and Other Early Christian Literature,* University of Chicago Press, 1952, p. 887.

13. Mahoney, Fr. John, S. J. "Dialogue between the Secretariat for Promoting Christian Unity of the Roman Catholic Church and Leaders of some Pentecostal Churches and Participants in the Charismatic Movement within Protestant and Anglican Churches," Venice, Italy, May 21-26, 1975. In discussion.

14. Harper, Michaie. *As At the Beginning, the Twentieth Century Pentecostal Revival,* Logos International, Plainfield, N.J., pp. 51-63.

15. Christenson, Larry. "Thoughts on Charismatic Renewal in the Lutheran Church," Unpublished paper presented in LCUSA theological consultation, p. 3.

16. See titles of church studies: "The Charismatic Movement in the LCA," "The Charismatic Movement and Lutheran Theology," "Theological and Pastoral Orientations on the Catholic Charismatic Renewal."

17. Voigt, Robert J. *Go to the Mountain,* Abbey Press, St. Meinard, Indiana, 1975, p. 34.

18. Tappert, Theodore G., editor and translator. *The Book of Concord,* Fortress Press, Philadelphia, PA., 1959, p. 345.

19. Wisloff, Fredrik. *I Believe in the Holy Spirit,* Augsburg Publishing House, Minneapolis, 1949, pp. 238, 239, 240.

20. Douglas, J. D., editor. *Let the Earth Hear His Voice,* Section entitled, "The Holy Spirit in the Charismatic Renewal of the Church" (Official Reference Volume of the International Congress on World Evangelization), World Wide Publications, Minneapolis, 1975, p. 1150.

21. Hollenweger, W. J. *The Pentecostals,* Augsburg Publishing House, Minneapolis, 1972, p. 236. While most Pentecostal groups consider speaking in tongues as the "initial evidence" of baptism with the Holy Spirit, Hollenweger points out exceptions.

22. Douglas, J. D., *op. cit.,* p. 1151. It is interesting to note the definite distinction drawn between the regenerating work of the Holy Spirit in baptism, and the empowering work of the Holy Spirit when people are baptized with the Holy Spirit, which was made by Dr. Jacob Tanner in his little tract, "Baptism: A Ceremony? Or, a Means of Grace?" His exegesis is similar to classical Pentecostalism at this point. *Book Mission Tract No. 137,* The Book Mission of the Evangelical Lutheran Church, Minneapolis, pp. 9-11.

23. Dayton, Donald W. "From Christian Perfection to the Bap-

tism of the Holy Ghost," article in *Aspects of Pentecostal-Charismatic Origins,* edited by Vinson Synan, Logos International, Plainfield, N.J., 1975, p. 51.

24. Suenens, Leon Joseph Cardinal. *A New Pentecost?* The Seabury Press, New York, 1974, pp. 83-86. See also: Bittlinger, Arnold. "Baptized in Water and Spirit." (Leaflet Evangel. No. B-2), Commission on Evangelism, ALC, 1972, 24 pages. —Christenson, Larry. "What About Baptism?" Bethany Fellowship, Inc., Minneapolis, 1973, pp. 18-21—"Malines Document." *Theological and Pastoral Orientations on the Catholic Charismatic Renewal,* Word of Life Publication, Notre Dame, Indiana, 1974, pp. 30-31.

25. Lazareth, William. In open forum at National Leaders' Conference for Lutheran Charismatic Renewal, Ann Arbor, Michigan, February 12, 1974. See also Tappert, *op. cit.,* p. 415.

26. Jensen, Richard A. *Touched by the Spirit,* Augsburg Publishing House, Minneapolis, 1975, pp. 108-109.

27. Wietzke, Walter and Hustad, Jack, editors. *Towards a Mutual Understanding of Neo-Pentecostalism,* Augsburg Publishing House, Minneapolis, 1973. See especially the article by Charles Robinson, an ALC pastor, titled, "Baptism with the Holy Spirit," pp. 19-30, in which he quotes extensively from the Lutheran Confessions. We cite two references: "Article II (Original Sin): 'It is taught among us that since the fall of Adam all men who are born according to the course of nature are conceived and born in sin ... Moreover, this inborn sickness and hereditary sin is truly sin and condemns to the eternal wrath of God all those who are not born again through Baptism and the Holy Spirit,' Part II, Solid Declaration of the Formula of Concord, Article II (Free Will, ref. no. 55): 'We cannot pass judgment on the Holy Spirit's presence, operations, and gifts merely on the basis of our feeling, how and when we perceive it in our hearts. On the contrary, because the Holy Spirit's activity often is hidden, and happens under cover of great weakness, we should be certain, because of and on the basis of his promise, that the Word which is heard and preached is an office and work of the Holy Spirit, whereby he assuredly is potent and active in our hearts (2 Co. 2:14ff).' "

28. See "Team Manual for the Life in the Spirit Seminars," Charismatic Renewal Services, Notre Dame, Indiana, 1971, pp. 82-89. This book is used throughout the Roman Catholic Charismatic Renewal to introduce people to the renewal. The

goal of the Fifth Lesson, cited here, is stated as follows: "To help them make an authentic commitment to Christ, to help them to be baptized in the Spirit and speak in tongues." Though the theological rationale is different from classical Pentecostalism, the similarity in experience and expectation is plain. See also Williams, J. Rodman, *op. cit.,* 20-26—Christenson, Larry. *Speaking in Tongues and Its Significance for the Church,* Bethany Fellowship, Inc., Minneapolis, 1968, pp. 33-40.

29. Tappert, *op. cit.,* p. 415.
30. *Ibid.,* p. 416.
31. *Ibid.,* p. 105.
32. Luther, Martin. *Luther's Works, Vol. 35, Word And Sacrament,* edited by E. Theodore Bachmann. Muhlenberg Press, Philadelphia, 1960, pp. 30-31.
33. It is interesting at this point to take note of a particular Roman Catholic interpretation. Francis Sullivan, a Jesuit scholar, adds a nuance to the standard Catholic sacramental interpretation: "St. Thomas asks the question whether one can speak of a sending of the Holy Spirit to a person in whom he is already indwelling, and if so, how this is to be understood. His answer is as follows: 'There is an invisible sending (of the Divine Person not only in the initial gift of grace but) also with respect to an advance in virtue or an increase of grace. . . . Such an invisible sending is especially to be seen in that kind of increase of grace whereby a person moves forward into some new act or some new state of grace: as, for example, when a person moves forward into the grace of working miracles, or of prophecy, or out of the burning love of God offers life as a martyr, or renounces all his possessions, or undertakes some other such heroic act' (*Summa* I, q. 43, a. 6, ad 2). What I found surprising when I first read this text is that when St. Thomas comes to give examples of such 'new acts or states of grace,' he does not speak of the effects of Confirmation or Holy Orders, as I would have expected him to do. Rather, he speaks of 'going forward' into the grace of working miracles, or of prophecy, or of martyrdom, or a total renunciation of worldly goods. All of these fall under the heading of 'charismatic,' rather than 'sacramental' graces." Taken from *Baptism in the Holy Spirit: A Catholic Interpretation of the Pentecostal Experience.* Gregorian University Press, Rome, 1974, pp. 52-53.
34. Note how this is expressed in Lutheran confirmation liturgy: "In Holy Baptism you were received by our Lord Jesus Christ

and made a member of his holy Church . . . may the Father in Heaven, for Jesus' sake, *renew and increase in thee the gift of the Holy Spirit.*" Service Book and Hymnal, Augsburg Publishing House, Minneapolis, 1958, p. 246.

35. Jensen, *op. cit.,* p. 123. See also: Bruner, Frederich D. *A Theology of the Holy Spirit,* William B. Eerdmans, Grand Rapids, Michigan, 1970, pp. 167, 178, 190, 197; Krodel, Gerhard. "The Spirit of God, Biblical Foundations," unpublished paper presented in LCUSA theological consultation," p. 38; Schlink, Edmund. *The Doctrine of Baptism,* Concordia Publishing House, St. Louis, Missouri, 1972, pp. 58-59.

36. Krodel, *op. cit.,* p. 37.

37. *Ibid.*

38. Wisloff, *op. cit.,* p. 240. See also: Dunn, James D. G. *Baptism in the Holy Spirit,* SCM Press, London, 1970.

39. Bruner, *op. cit.,* p. 178.

40. Hollenweger, *op. cit.,* p. 337.

41. Various attempts have been made to explain the variations in the several accounts in which the coming of the Holy Spirit is recorded in *Acts* (especially chapters 8, 10, and 19), in order to fit them into a particular theological framework. Classical Pentecostals go through and interpret every text to support their theology of "baptism with the Holy Spirit with the initial evidence of speaking in tongues." Frederick Bruner uses the same methodology to support exactly opposite conclusions. Fundamentalists (and, interestingly, some historical-critical exegetes) make a strong link between the three part "outline" in Acts 1:8, and the unique, unrepeatable outpourings of the Spirit in 2, 8, and 10. Every form of systematization seems to have trouble fitting at least one of the texts into its system: Pentecostals have trouble with 19, non-Pentecostals with 8, and fundamentalists with 19. The text itself offers no clear explanation for the variations; we are left with a degree of uncertainty. We are perhaps on safer ground to recognize in these variations a sovereign action of God, than to try to fit them into a tenuous system.

42. Conzelman, Hans. "Die Apostelgeschichte," *Handbuch Zum Neuen Testament,* J. C. B. Mohr (Paul Siebeck), Tuebingen, Germany, 1963, p. 55.

43. Krodel, *op. cit.,* p. 38.

44. Burnett, William. In lecture at Second International Conference on the Holy Spirit, Jerusalem, November 3, 1975.

45. McDonnell, Kilian. In private correspondence.

46. Du Plessis, David. "Jesus Christ the Baptizer in the Holy Spirit," privately published tract, 3742 Linwood Avenue, Oakland, California.

47. Hogan, Joseph. "Charismatic Renewal in the Catholic Church: An Evaluation." *New Covenant*, September 1971, p. 2.

48. Schmid, Heinrich. *Doctrinal Theology of the Evangelical Lutheran Church*, Lutheran Publication Society, Philadelphia, 1875, p. 537. See also: Luther, Martin. *op. cit.*

49. Bittlinger, *op. cit.*

50. Tappert, *op. cit.*, p. 535.

51. See footnote 24.

52. Hollenweger, *op. cit.*, see pp. 236-237 for reference to a minority of Pentecostals who did not hold to the doctrine of "initial evidence."

53. Christenson, *Speaking in Tongues, op. cit.*, p. 54. See also: Malines Document, *op. cit.*, p. 53.—Clark, Stephen. *Baptized in the Spirit,* Dove Publications, Pecos, New Mexico, 1970, p. 26.

54. Synan, Vinson. *The Holiness-Pentecostal Movement in the United States.* William B. Eerdmans Publishing Company, Grand Rapids, Michigan, 1971, pp. 153-158. Dr. Synan here presents the history of the so-called "oneness Doctrine," a controversy over baptism which took place in the Pentecostal Movement between 1913 and 1916; it never gained a wide foothold in Pentecostal circles.

55. Barth, Karl. *The Teaching of the Church Regarding Baptism,* SCM Press, London, 1948.

56. Boehm, Karl. *Lights and Shadows in the Present Condition of the Church,* Thomas Bosworth, London, 1874, pp. 102-103.

57. Schlink, Edmund. *The Doctrine of Baptism,* Concordia Publishing House, St. Louis, Missouri, 1972, p. 130.

58. Boehm, *op. cit.*, p. 96.

59. Kallas, James. *The Satanward View,* The Westminster Press, Philadelphia, Pennsylvania, 1966, pp. 101-102.

60. Deuteronomy 18:15.

61. Klingman, John A. *Luther on Baptism,* F. L. Rowe, Cincinatti, Ohio, 1913, p. 23.

62. Schlink, *op. cit.*, p. 136.

63. Every, George. Author of, *The Baptsmal Sacrifice,* in a seminar at Nottingham University, England, July 11, 1973.

64. Anderson, Paul. "Infant Baptism: A Study of the Lutheran

and Baptist Positions," unpublished manuscript by B. D. candidate, Luther Theological Seminary, St. Paul, Minnesota, 1972, p. 17.

65. Schlink, *op. cit.*, p. 132.

66. *Ibid.*, p. 133.

67. Boehm, *op. cit.*, pp. 113-114.

68. Schlink, *op. cit.*, p. 136.

69. Ranaghan, Kevin. "The Problem of Re-Baptism," *Pastoral Newsletter*, Ann Arbor, Michigan, p. 6.

70. Klingman, *op. cit.*, pp. 5-6.

71. Prenter, Regin. *Spiritus Creator*, Fortress Press, Philadelphia, 1953, pp. 169, 48, 61. See also: von Loewenich, Walther. *Luther's Theology of the Cross*, Augsburg Publishing House, Minneapolis, 1976, pp. 83-101.

72. Tappert, *op. cit.*, p. 43.

73. *The Work of the Holy Spirit*, Report to the 182nd General Assembly of the United Presbyterian Church. Office of the General Assembly, 510 Witherspoon Building, Philadelphia, Pennsylvania 19107, 1970, p. 15.

74. Malines Document, *op. cit.*, p. 23, where it is pointed out that Roman Catholics also are generally unfamiliar with the peak or crisis-type experience.

75. Bonhoeffer, Dietrich. "A Wedding Sermon From a Cell," *Letters and Papers From Prison*, The Macmillan Company, New York, 1967.

76. McDonnell, Kilian, In open form at theological conference in Rome, May 19, 1975.

77. Wietzke, Walter. *The American Lutheran Church and Neo-Pentecostalism, an Interpretive Resource for Pastors*, The American Lutheran Church, Minneapolis, 1975, p. 1.

78. Bainton, Roland, *Here I Stand*, Abingdon Press, New York & Nashville, 1950, p. 361.

79. Christenson, Larry. *Social Action—Jesus Style*. Bethany Fellowship, Inc., Minneapolis, 1974, pp. 12-15.

80. McDonnell, Kilian. "The Catholic Charismatic Renewal: Reassessment and Critique," *Religion in Life*, Summer, 1975, Vol. XLIV, No. 2.

81. Hollenweger, *op. cit.*, p. 7, where he notes the widespread influence of David du Plessis.

82. Du Plessis, David, in private conversation.

83. Malines Document, *op. cit.*, p. 42.

84. *Ibid.*, pp. 17-18.

85. *Ibid.*

86. *Ibid.,* p. 42.
87. Christenson, Larry. *Speaking in Tongues, op. cit.* The extended section on Speaking in Tongues is adapted in large measure from the author's previous book on the subject.
88. This is the conclusion of the study of Gerlach and Hine, which looked at the Pentecostal/charismatic phenomena from the standpoint of cultural anthropology. *Journal for the Scientific Study of Religion* 7/1, Spring 1968.
89. McDonnell, Kilian. *Catholic Pentecostalism: Problems in Evaluation,* Dove Publications, Pecos, New Mexico, 1970, p. 19.
90. Wietzke, *Toward a Mutual Understanding,* etc., *op. cit.,* p. 8.
91. *The Relation of the Christian Faith to Health,* report adopted by the 172nd General Assembly of the United Presbyterian Church, May 1960, pp. 15-16.
92. Sanford, Edgar. *The Healing Power of God,* Prentice-Hall, Englewood Cliffs, New Jersey, 1959, pp. 4-5.
93. Guidelines followed at Trinity Lutheran Church (ALC), San Pedro, California.
94. Froelich, Karlfried. "Biblical and Confessional Aspects of Charismatic Manifestations," unpublished paper presented in LCUSA Theological Consultation, p. 16.
95. *Ibid.,* pp. 16-17.
96. Luther, Martin. "Treatise on Good Works." Holman Edition, Vol. I, Philadelphia, p. 201. See also Luther's commentary on *Galatians,* edited by Philip S. Watson, Fleming H. Revell, Westwood, New Jersey, pp. 343, 344, 142, 168, 170.
97. "Report of the Committee on Doctrine of the National Conference of Catholic Bishops submitted to the Bishops in their meeting in Washington, D.C., November 14, 1969. The report was presented by Bishop Alexander Zaleski of Lansing, Michigan, Chairman of the Committee."
98. Christenson, Larry. "Don't Set Your Congregation on Its Ear." *Loaves and Fishes,* July 1972, p. 1.
99. Motto of the "Ruferbewegung."
100. *Event Magazine,* November-December, 1973, p. 36.
101. Christenson, *Speaking in Tongues, op. cit.,* pp. 104-106.
102. McDonnell, *Religion in Life, op. cit.*
103. Private information.
104. Forrest, Tom. In forum at International Catholic Leaders' Conference, Rome, May 12, 1975.
105. Jensen, *op. cit.,* p. 79.

106. *Lutheran Charismatic Renewal Newsletter*, Box 14344, University Station, Minneapolis, Minnesota, Vol. i, No. 1, November 1974, p. 4.
107. McDonnell, Kilian. In open forum at World Council of Churches Assembly, Nairobi, Kenya, East Africa, November 26, 1975.